SMALL CLAIMS COURT GUIDE
FOR BRITISH COLUMBIA

SMALL CLAIMS COURT GUIDE FOR BRITISH COLUMBIA

How to win your case!

Kathleen Keating, LL.B.

Self-Counsel Press
(*a division of*)
International Self-Counsel Press Ltd.
Canada   U.S.A.

Printed in Canada

First edition: October, 1971
Second edition: September, 1972
Third edition: September, 1974
Fourth edition: December, 1977
Fifth edition: June, 1979
Sixth edition: January, 1981
Seventh edition: November, 1983
Eighth edition: December, 1986
Ninth edition: September, 1992

Canadian Cataloguing in Publication Data
Keating, Kathleen, 1949-
    Small Claims Court guide for British Columbia
    (Self-counsel legal series)
    First-2nd eds., by Patrick Good, published under title: Layman's guide to Small Claims Court; 3rd-7th eds. published under title: Small Claims Court guide for British Columbia; 8th ed. published under title: Small Claim Court guide for British Columbia; 3rd-6th eds. by Heather Fayers; 7th-8th eds. by Juhli Anten.
ISBN 0-88908-458-01.
    Small claims courts—British Columbia—Popular works.
    I. Title. II. Title: Small Claim Court guide for British Columbia.
    III. Series.   KEB538.Z82K42 1992   347.711'04   C92-091313-X
    KF8737.A75K42 1992

Self-Counsel Press
(a division of)
International Self-Counsel Press Ltd.
Head and Editorial Office
1481 Charlotte Road
North Vancouver, British Columbia V7J 1H1

U.S. Address
1704 N. State Street
Bellingham, Washington 98225

CONTENTS

SAMPLES

NOTICE TO READERS

Laws are constantly changing. Every effort is made to keep this publication as current as possible. However, neither the author nor the publisher can accept any responsibility for changes to the law or practice that occur after the printing of this publication. Please be sure that you have the most recent edition.

Note: The fees quoted in this book are correct at the date of publication. However, fees are subject to change without notice. For current fees, please check with the court registry or appropriate government office nearest you.

1

BEFORE YOU BEGIN

a. WHAT IS SMALL CLAIMS COURT?

The Small Claims Court of British Columbia is intended as a place where people can go to resolve disputes fairly, quickly, and inexpensively, without the cost of hiring lawyers. The official name of the Small Claims Court is the Provincial Court of British Columbia, Civil Division. (**Note:** throughout this book I use the common name, Small Claims Court.) The judges who sit in Small Claims Court also hear criminal, family court, and juvenile cases — sometimes in the same day in the same courtroom.

You may hire a lawyer to represent you if you wish, but the forms, procedures and rules are all designed with the non-lawyer in mind. The small claims process is also designed to encourage settlement of disputes, without the necessity of a trial in every case. You will read more about settlement conferences and the other opportunities for settlement that the Small Claims Court provides later in this book.

This book explains how to use the forms and proceed through a small claims action, whether or not it goes to trial. It is designed to provide a simple, yet complete, guide to using the facilities of Small Claims Court to either make a claim or defend an action.

1. Some words to know

The Small Claims Court Rules were written with the layperson in mind and you shouldn't have any difficulty understanding the language used in the rules or in this book. But there are a few words and phrases that you may not be familiar with in this context. The three terms used most often are —

(a) **Claimant:** The person who starts the lawsuit by making a claim.

(b) **Defendant:** The person against whom a claim is made.

(c) **Service of documents:** Giving documents to another party in a lawsuit, according to the rules of the court.

See the Glossary at the back of the book for explanations of other words and phrases that may be unfamiliar.

b. WHAT CASES DOES SMALL CLAIMS COURT HANDLE?

1. Dollar limit

If you are wondering whether your case belongs in Small Claims Court, the first thing to know is that the upper limit is $10 000. This limit includes the total value of everything you are claiming, whether it is money or goods or services, and whether your claim is against one or more defendants. However, it does not include any claim for interest or for reimbursement for expenses such as your filing fee.

This means that even if your claim is for $10 000, you may claim the full amount, plus reimbursement for expenses such as your filing fee.

If your claim is for more than $10 000, you may still use the Small Claims Court if you wish, but you must abandon your claim for the excess amount.

Suppose, for example, that you have a claim against someone for $11 500 but you want to handle the case yourself in Small Claims Court. You may reduce your claim to $10 000 plus interest and costs, as long as you abandon your claim for the extra $1 500.

If your claim is for more than $10 000 and you don't want to reduce the amount, you must use the Supreme Court, which has no dollar limit. There, procedures are more formal and more complicated and you are likely to need the services of a lawyer. Keep this in mind if you are unsure whether to abandon part of your claim or not in order to meet the dollar limit of Small Claims Court. If you are saving the cost of hiring a lawyer to represent you in Supreme Court, it may be worth your while.

If you do abandon part of your claim, you cannot sue for that part separately, in Small Claims or any other court. That part of your claim is gone. There is only one exception to this rule:

Example:

A contractor invoices a homeowner for $11 000 and the homeowner does not pay. The contractor decides to abandon $1 000 of the claim and sues for $10 000 plus interest in Small Claims Court. The homeowner believes that the contractor's poor workmanship has caused $15 000 worth of damage to her home. She sues the contractor in Supreme Court for $15 000. Even though the contractor abandoned part of his claim in Small Claims Court, he may now counterclaim in Supreme Court for the full $11 000 of the invoice.

2. Cases allowed

Small Claims Court is designed to handle certain types of cases, particularly —

(a) claims for debt (someone owes you a specific amount of money); or

(b) claims for damages (you want someone to pay for an injury or loss you have suffered).

Other types of cases that may be brought in Small Claims Court are:

(a) claims for recovery of personal property (someone has something that belongs to you and you want it back);

(b) claims for specific performance of an agreement relating to personal property or to personal services (someone agreed to do something and you want the court to order him or her to do it);

(c) claims for relief from opposing claims to personal property (you have possession of an item and two different people claim ownership of it).

3. Cases not allowed

As stated before, only claims for up to $10 000 may be brought in Small Claims Court. But some types of cases may never be brought in Small Claims Court, no matter how much money is involved. These include the following:

(a) Landlord and tenant

Landlord and tenant disputes are handled by the Residential Tenancy Branch. The Branch's address and telephone numbers can be found in the blue pages of the telephone book under the provincial government listings.

(b) Real property

Small Claims Court cannot hear any claim relating to ownership of real property. "Real property" includes land, houses, condominiums — everything that most people refer to as "real estate." Even if you were claiming damages of less than $10 000, you would have to go to Supreme Court. The same applies to builders' liens claims.

(c) Libel, slander, and malicious prosecution

Small Claims Court cannot hear any claim for libel, slander, or malicious prosecution. If you want to sue someone for saying or publishing untrue things about you, you must do that in Supreme Court.

c.   HOW MUCH DOES IT COST?

One of the goals of the Small Claims Court is to provide an inexpensive way of resolving claims. If you are making a claim, you will have to pay a $25 filing fee when you begin your action. (If you are the defendant in a case, there is no filing fee.) From then on, how much you spend depends on you and your situation. (**Note:** Fees were accurate at the time of printing. Call the Small Claims Court to verify current fees.)

For example, you might pay a professional document server (called a "process server") to deliver your Notice of Claim to the defendant. If so, the charges will depend on the distance involved and the time it takes. Don't hesitate to get a fee quotation from more than one process server. When you do, be sure to say that it is a Small Claims document you want served. Many servers charge lower rates for these. Also, confirm that the fee quoted includes the cost of completing the certificate of service that you will need.

Or, you might serve the document yourself, at no cost. In some cases you might have to pay an expert to prepare a report for you to use in evidence, or to testify in court. In other cases, the witnesses may agree to testify without charge. Or, there may be no witnesses other than the claimant and defendant themselves.

If you are successful in your claim, the judge may order the other party to reimburse you for your reasonable expenses. This would include your filing fee (if you were the claimant) and any money you spent on the case, so long as it was reasonable. For example, it might be reasonable to pay a mileage charge for a witness to drive from Terrace to Smithers to testify for you. You might get an order that the other side pay you for that expense. On the other hand, if you hire a chauffeured limousine to bring your witness to court, you would likely be stuck with that expense yourself, whether you win or lose the case.

If the defendant makes a counterclaim (i.e., a claim against the claimant) and is even partially successful, the court will likely order that each side pay its own costs.

If you hire a lawyer, you will not recover that expense from the other side, no matter how successful you are, as the Small Claims Act does not allow it.

The forms provided by the Small Claims Court are free except to those who act on behalf of others for a fee, such as lawyers and collection agencies.

d. HOW LONG DOES IT TAKE?

The length of time it will take to resolve your claim will depend on several factors, including the following:

(a) How busy the court is (this will vary from one location to another);

(b) Whether you can find the defendant and serve your documents without delay;

(c) Whether the defendant disputes the claim; and

(d) Whether one or both sides are willing to compromise in order to reach a settlement.

If the defendant does not dispute the claim and can be served easily, the claimant can have judgment 14 days after service of the Notice of Claim. However, if the defendant disputes the claim, a court date will be set. When that will be depends on the court's schedule.

If you want to know how far ahead dates are being set at your court location, ask a clerk at the court registry.

e. TIME LIMITS

The right to sue someone does not last forever. The law imposes time limits (called "limitation periods") on legal rights. After the limitation period has expired, you cannot begin a lawsuit, so it is important not to delay too long. Different limitation periods apply to different kinds of actions, but these are some general rules:

(a) Actions for damages as a result of an automobile accident: two years from the date of the accident, or one year if you are suing the Insurance Corporation of British Columbia (ICBC);

(b) Actions for unpaid debts: six years from the date the debt was incurred or from the time the debtor last acknowledged the debt. (For example, if you lent someone some money in 1989 and he or she made monthly payments until 1991, you would have until 1997 to sue for the balance.)

You must begin most other actions for damages within two years from the date the damage occurred. However, there are many exceptions, especially when the defendant is a government body or a professional person.

Even though you may want to settle a dispute in some other way, if there is any chance you may want to sue, don't delay too long. If you are unsure about your limitation period, get advice from one of the people or agencies listed in section **g.** below.

Remember that it is almost always easier to prove a claim that is brought before the court promptly. With time, witnesses' memories fade, evidence is lost, and documents go missing.

f. USING THE SMALL CLAIMS COURT RULES, FORMS, AND BOOKLETS

The rules that govern Small Claims Court are in plain language, printed in an easy-to-read format with a complete table of contents. You can get a copy at any provincial court registry.

Special forms are provided for use in Small Claims Court. They are multi-part forms with different copies for different purposes. For example, the Notice of Claim has one copy for the court records, one for the claimant to keep, one for the defendant to keep, and one to attach to the certificate proving that the document was properly served. Always make sure that you have the appropriate copy of each form because the instructions and information they contain can vary. (See Sample #1 in chapter 2.)

If you need extra copies of a form — to serve several defendants, for example — you may use photocopies. Be sure that they are duplicates of the appropriate copy of the form.

To fill in the forms you may use a typewriter or print with a ballpoint pen. You also may use a computer and impact printer if you have software that allows you to fill in forms. Whatever you use, be sure all copies are readable.

There is also a series of booklets supplied by the court to explain the major steps in the process. If you are acting on your own behalf or for your own company, you can get these booklets and forms free of charge from any Small Claims Court registry. If there is not a registry near you, your government agent may have them.

If you are acting on behalf of others (e.g., for a collection agent), you may obtain a supply of forms from a commercial stationer.

g. WHERE TO GO FOR MORE HELP

If you feel you need some help before you start your claim, there are a number of places where you can get legal advice for little or no charge.

1. DIAL-A-LAW

DIAL-A-LAW is a project of the Canadian Bar Association, B.C. Branch. It is a library of pre-recorded taped messages on a variety of legal topics, available by telephone 24 hours a day, 7 days a week. All you need is a touch-tone telephone. (From a rotary dial phone you must call during regular office hours.) The number to call in the Greater Vancouver area is 687-4680. Outside the Vancouver calling area, the toll-free number is 1-800-972-0956. These tapes are prepared by B.C. lawyers to provide practical information; several deal specifically with Small Claims Court.

2. Lawyer referral

If you would like to talk to a lawyer about your problem, or get advice about whether to use the Small Claims Court, you might try the Lawyer Referral Service, also operated by the Bar Association. The telephone number for the Lawyer Referral office in your area is listed in the yellow pages of your telephone directory under "Lawyers." In Vancouver and the lower mainland the number is 687-3221. When you call, tell the operator the general nature of your problem and you will be given the name of a lawyer. You arrange an appointment with that lawyer and tell him or her that the Lawyer Referral Service referred you. The lawyer will see you for up to 30 minutes for a fee of $10.

3. Law student clinics

In the Greater Vancouver area the Law Students Legal Advice Program staffs clinics with law students who give free advice to people who would not be able to afford a lawyer. For more information, call 228-5791.

4. Court registry

The staff behind the counter at the Small Claims Court registries cannot give you legal advice, but they are experienced in small claims rules and procedures and are very helpful.

h. WHERE TO FIND YOUR SMALL CLAIMS COURT

Small Claims registries are located throughout the province. Before deciding where to begin your action, read chapter 2, which explains the rules about where a claim must be filed. The Appendix at the back of this book lists the locations of all registries in the province.

i. SUMMARY

Before beginning a small claims action, these are some of the things you should consider:

(a) How much is your claim worth — if it is over $10 000 should you abandon the excess amount or go to Supreme Court and claim the full amount?

(b) Is yours one of the types of claims that Small Claims Court can hear?

(c) Has the time limit for bringing your claim expired?

After reading through this book, if you need more help or advice, consult one of the agencies listed earlier.

Finally, take a look at what you are claiming, your chances of winning, and — maybe most important — your chances of collecting from the defendant if you do win your case. Small Claims Court procedures are as simple as they can be. But a court case will still take your time and may cause you worry and stress. And although there are enforcement procedures for you to use, trying to collect from a defendant who cannot or will not pay can be an exercise in frustration. Only you can decide whether your claim is worth taking to court.

2
GETTING STARTED

a. NOTICE OF CLAIM

The Notice of Claim is the document that begins a Small Claims Court action (see Sample #1). It names the claimant and defendant and tells what the claim is about. It also tells the defendant what to do next.

Get a form from any Small Claims Court registry (or your government agent if there isn't a registry near you) and read the instructions carefully. If it isn't convenient to go to a registry, you can call or write and have the form sent to you. See the Appendix at the back of the book for addresses and phone numbers.

At the same time, you should get a copy of the free booklet "Making a Claim." If you're interested in the Small Claims Rules themselves, you can also get a free copy of those at the registry. The rules about the Notice of Claim are found in Rule 1.

1. Identifying the claimant

If you are the claimant it will be a simple matter to give your own full name. If you have a limited company you will have to consider whether to name yourself or the company (or both) as claimant.

If you are claiming an amount due under a contract, then the proper claimant will be the party named in the contract. If the contract was with you personally, then you will be the claimant. If it was between the defendant and your company, the company is the proper claimant.

SAMPLE #1
NOTICE OF CLAIM

NOTICE OF CLAIM

NOTICE OF CLAIM

IN THE PROVINCIAL COURT OF BRITISH COLUMBIA (SMALL CLAIMS COURT)

FORM 1 (RULE 1)
SCL 201.11 90-

REGISTRY FILE NUMBER
45678*
REGISTRY LOCATION
Prince George

FROM:
Fill in the name, address and telephone number of the person(s) or business(es) making the claim.

NAME Robin Gardiner
ADDRESS 123 King Street

CITY, TOWN MUNICIPALITY Prince George   B.C. PROV   V6K 1L7 POSTAL CODE   TEL. 269-1234

CLAIMANT(S)

TO:
Fill in the name, address and telephone number of the person(s) or business(es) the claim is against.

NAME Leslie Householder
ADDRESS 789 Main Street

CITY, TOWN MUNICIPALITY Prince George   B.C. PROV   V6K 2M3 POSTAL CODE   TEL. 379-5678

DEFENDANT(S)

WHAT HAPPENED?
Tell what led to the claim.

I agreed to cut the Defendant's lawn once a week for June, July, and August, 199-, and the Defendant agreed to pay me $20.00 per cut. I cut the lawn as agreed but the Defendant has not paid.

My last invoice, dated September 30, 199-, was for $240.00 and it is still unpaid.

WHERE?
Tell where this happened.

CITY, TOWN MUNICIPALITY Prince George, B.C. PROV

WHEN?
Tell when this happened.

September 30, 199-

HOW MUCH?
Tell what is being claimed from the defendant(s). If the claim is made up of several parts, separate them here and show the amount for each part. Add these amounts and fill in the total claimed.

a Invoice #678, dated September 30, 199 $ 240 00

b Interest under the Court Order Interest Act $

c $

d $

e $

Sign here

Robin Gardiner
SIGNATURE OF CLAIMANT

TOTAL   240 00

TIME LIMIT FOR A DEFENDANT
If a defendant does not settle directly with the claimant or file a reply **within 14 days**, a court order may be made against the defendant. Then the defendant will have to pay the amount claimed plus interest and further expenses.

The Court Address for filing documents is:

The court registry staff will fill in these figures

\+ FILING FEES

\+ SERVICE FEES

= TOTAL CLAIMED $ **

DEBT
OTHER THAN DEBT

court copy

court copy

NOTICE OF CLAIM

---

*This number will be assigned and filled in by the registry for use on all subsequent documents.
**Leave this total blank; it is calculated on the basis of the final order.

If you are claiming for damages to property, the owner of the property is the proper claimant. For example, if you are claiming that the defendant ran into your car, then you are the claimant. If you say the defendant ran into the truck owned by your company, then the company is the claimant. If you suffered loss or injury personally, then you would also be a claimant, along with the company.

Be sure to insert your correct address. This is where the court and the defendant will send notices and other mail to you. If you move, make sure to let the court and all other parties know your new address right away. If you don't, something might happen in your case, and you might not be notified about it.

2. Identifying the defendant

Naming the defendant correctly can be tricky, especially if the defendant is a business. If you get it wrong, you could end up with a judgment against a defendant who does not exist. Or, you could win your case but find that the assets you thought would be available to pay you belong to someone else (e.g., the defendant's company).

(a) Individuals

If the defendant is one or more individuals, you shouldn't have a problem. Use whole names as far as possible, as opposed to initials. Do not use titles such as Mr., Mrs., Ms., or Dr. If there are two defendants, use both full names even if they have the same last name. For example, say Joe Smith and Mary Smith (*not* Mr. and Mrs. Joe Smith or Joe and Mary Smith).

(b) Businesses

If you are suing a defendant who operates through a business that is not incorporated, you should sue both the person and the business. That way, if you are successful you will be able to collect your judgment against either of them. This is the proper way to name them:

Joe Smith carrying on business as Smith Auto Company, and Smith Auto Company

Note that the word "company" does not necessarily mean that the business is incorporated, or is a limited company. You may use the abbreviation "c.o.b.a." for "carrying on business as."

To find the proper name of an unincorporated business, contact the business licence office of the municipality where the business is located. They will give you the correct name of the business and the person or corporation that holds the business licence. This is usually the proprietor (owner) of the business, though not always.

(c) Companies

If you are suing a limited company, you must use the full name and it must be accurate. A limited company will have one of these words as part of its name:

(a) Limited

(b) Ltd.

(c) Incorporated

(d) Inc.

(e) Corporation

(f) Corp.

If you are suing a limited company, write to the registrar of companies in Victoria and ask for a full company search. This will give you the correct name of the company as well as the address of the company's registered office and other information you may need later on. The address is —

Registrar of Companies
940 Blanshard Street
Victoria, B.C.
V8W 2H3

Send a cheque or money order for $6 payable to the Minister of Finance. You can also telephone the registry in Victoria at 387-5101.

One of the features of a limited company is that the owners' liability is limited to the amount of their ownership in the company. For example, say you win a lawsuit against Smith Cleaners Ltd. You find that the company owns no assets except some mops and brooms. However, the company's two shareholders, Joe and Mary Smith, own a large home and two cars. You have no claim against the house and cars. If the company doesn't pay the judgment, you could try seizing assets, but only those owned by the company itself.

That is why, when dealing with small companies, many banks and others try to get personal guarantees from the company's owners. That way, the person can be sued as well as the company.

The address of the company is the registered address as shown in your company search. This very often is not the same as the address where the company carries on business.

(d) Accident cases

If you are suing for the deductible portion of your insurance as a result of a motor vehicle accident, you should name both the driver and the registered owner of the vehicle as defendants. If you have the licence number of the vehicle you can get the owner's name by writing a letter to the Vehicle Records Office of ICBC (see Sample #2). The fee is currently $15.

3. What happened?

In this part you will tell, as clearly and as briefly as you can, what happened that led you to sue. The following are some examples to help you. You should use your own words.

John Doe
123 Any Street
Vancouver, B.C.
V6C 1T2

Vehicle Records Office
Insurance Corporation of B.C.
151 W. Esplanade
North Vancouver, B.C.
V7M 3H9

Dear Sir or Madam:
Re: B.C. 199_ Licence No. ___-___

Please send me a certified extract of ownership as of September 1, 199-
(the date of the accident) for the vehicle with this 199_ licence plate.

I enclose a cheque *(or money order)* for $15.00.

Yours truly,

John Doe

John Doe

(a) Money owing for goods sold

I sold (description of goods sold, for example: "a color television set") to the defendant. The price was $_____ and the defendant has not paid.

(b) Money owing for goods sold and delivered

I sold and delivered (description of goods) to the defendant. The price was $_____ and the defendant has not paid.

(c) Money owing for services rendered

I (description of services rendered, for example: washed all windows at the defendant's place of business) at the defendant's request. The price was $_____ and the defendant has not paid.

(d) Loan of money

I loaned $_____ to the defendant at her request. The loan was made on or about the ___ day of _____, 19__, at (place), British Columbia. The defendant has not paid. The particulars are:

(example)

Amount of loan:	$400
OR	
Amount of loan:	$400
Interest:	20
Total:	$420

(e) Balance owing on loan of money

I loaned $_____ to the defendant at her request. The loan was made on or about the ___ day of _____, 19__, at (place), British Columbia. The defendant has repaid $_____ but has not paid the balance. The particulars are:

(example)

Amount of loan	$400
Less payment:	10
BALANCE:	$390

(f) Dishonored cheques

The defendant gave me a cheque in the amount of $_____, drawn by the defendant on the (name and branch of bank), dated the ___ day of _____, 19__, payable to me. The cheque was delivered to me by the defendant for good and valuable consideration on the ___ day of _____, 19__. This cheque was dishonored by the bank and returned to me. The defendant has been told that the cheque was dishonored and has not paid.

(g) For goods purchased and not received

I paid the defendant $_____ on the ____ day of _____, 19__ at (place) as the purchase price for a freezer and color television set. The defendant has not supplied or delivered these goods.

(h) Suing on a judgment from another province

The defendant owes me $_____ as a result of Judgment No._____, obtained in the Court of_____ at (City)_____, in the Province of_____ on the ___ day of _____, 19__ in the amount of $_____. No payments have been made on this judgment.

(i) Improper repairs

The defendant breached a contract to repair my (e.g., motor vehicle) either by:

(a) failing to repair the (vehicle) in a proper and workmanlike manner; or

(b) negligently repairing the (vehicle).
Repairs were to be made at the defendant's place of business at _____. The contract was oral (or written) and it was made between me and the defendant on the ___ day of _____, 19__.
I have suffered damages in the amount of $_____ as a result of the defendant's breach of this contract.

(j) Suing on a promissory note

The defendant signed a promissory note in the amount of
$_____, dated the _____ day of _____, 19___ and delivered to
me on the ___ day of _____, 19__. I have demanded payment of the debt and the defendant has refused or neglected
to pay.

(k) Motor vehicle accident

(i) Where both drivers are also the owners

I suffered damages in the amount of $_____, as a result of a
motor vehicle accident caused by the negligence of the defendant. The accident happened on the ___ day of _____, 19__,
at _____ in the City of _____, British Columbia. A motor vehicle owned and negligently operated by
the defendant _____ collided with the motor vehicle
owned and operated by me.

(ii) Where both drivers are not the owners

I suffered damages in the amount of $_____, as a result of a
motor vehicle accident caused by the negligence of the defendant. The accident happened on the ___ day of _____, 19__,
at _____ in the City of _____, British Columbia. A motor vehicle owned by _____ and negligently operated by _____ collided with the motor
vehicle owned by _____ and operated by
_____ with the owner's express or implied consent.

(iii) Claim for deductible

I suffered damages as a result of a motor vehicle accident
caused by the defendant's negligence. The accident happened
on the ___ day of _____, 19__, at _____ in the
City of _____, British Columbia. A motor vehicle
owned by _____ and negligently operated by
_____ collided with the motor vehicle owned and
operated by _____. Total amount of the damages

caused by the accident was $_____. The unpaid amount I am claiming is $_____.

4. Where?

You may have already answered this question in section **3. *What happened***, but fill it in here anyway. You don't need a street address; just the city, town, or other place where it happened, and the province.

The registry staff then can easily see whether you are filing your claim in the correct registry.

The rules require you to file your claim EITHER:

(a) where the defendant lives or carries on business; or

(b) where the event that resulted in the claim happened.

The following examples show how the rule applies:

Example #1

You are suing over a car accident that happened in Burnaby. The other driver lives in Surrey and you live in Vancouver. You may file your claim in either Burnaby (where the event happened) or Surrey (where the defendant lives), but not in Vancouver.

Example #2

You operate a building supply business in Kamloops. A customer from Prince George comes into your store and pays for some windows with a cheque that is returned "NSF." You may file your claim in Prince George (where the defendant lives) or in Kamloops (where the transaction took place). But, if you go to Prince George to install the windows and he gives you the cheque there, you will have to file in Prince George UNLESS you can show that the contract was made in Kamloops.

If the registry staff notices that your claim ought to be filed in another registry, they will tell you. However, the responsibility is yours and if you make a mistake you may have to start over again. If the time has run out by then, you may lose your claim altogether.

(The court where you file your claim is not necessarily the place where every step in your case will take place. In chapter 8, Applications to Court, you will learn how to make an application to have your case heard at another court location.)

5. When?

Even if you have already given this information in the *What happened?* section, tell here when the event or transaction took place. Give the date or dates as exactly as you can. If you can't say the exact date with certainty then you may say "on or about" and give your best estimate.

The reason this information is requested here, is to let the registry staff quickly see whether your claim is being made on time. If they think it is not, they will let you know. However, ensuring that your claim is timely is not their responsibility — it is yours.

Most lawsuits have to be started within a certain time limit and it can be quite tricky in some cases to determine when the time starts to run and how long before it expires. Generally speaking, you have six years to sue on a debt and two years to sue for damages.

In Example #2 above, the window installer would have **six** years to sue the customer who failed to pay. But if the customer wanted to sue the contractor for negligently installing the windows, that lawsuit would have to be started within **two** years.

Sometimes there are complicated legal arguments about time limits. The results can be significant because if the time limit has expired, the legal right to sue is gone. The general rule is that if negotiations don't produce results quickly, start your action without delay. Just because you have filed a claim doesn't mean you have to do anything with it right away. You can wait up to a year before even giving it to the defendant. (See chapter 3.)

If you have any doubt at all about the time limit on your action, you should get legal advice. This may be an occasion to use the Lawyer Referral Service described in chapter 1.

6. How much?

This is where you tell what it is you want from the defendant. In most cases, this will be an amount of money, but it might be something else (e.g., the return of goods).

Often a claim will have more than one part. For example, you might be claiming a debt, plus interest. Or you might be claiming damages for several items. You should use the separate lines marked *a, b, c,* and so on, to list the parts of your claim.

For example, suppose you contracted with a plumber to install a new shower stall in your bathroom. You say he did the work negligently: the stall was cracked and it leaked into the room below and had to be replaced. You might list your claim like this:

a	Cost of replacing shower stall	$450
b	Cost of repairing ceiling below	$250
c	Cost of repairing bathroom floor	$220
TOTAL		$920

It would be unusual to have more than five parts. You may attach a separate piece of paper if you need to: just remember to make the right number of copies.

Put the amounts next to the dollar signs in the column at the right as shown in Sample #1. Put the total in the space indicated. When you take your Notice of Claim to the registry, the staff will fill in an amount for filing fees and service fees, and the final total.

(a) Interest

There are some rules about interest that you should know if you plan to claim it.

First, if you and the defendant had agreed on a rate of interest, then this is the rate you must claim, if you claim interest at all.

If you had no agreement about interest, or if you did but you make no claim for it, you are still entitled, if you win your case, to the interest rate provided by the Court Order Interest Act. The rate is generally quite low, but you don't need to worry about calculating the amount now. That will be done when you eventually file your payment order.

Any interest you do claim must be expressed as an annual rate. The Canada Interest Act says that (except in the case of mortgages) if you claim interest but don't state it as an annual rate, you are only entitled to 5% per annum.

If you are claiming interest, calculate the amount owing up to the date you file your Notice of Claim. Fill that in, then add a statement that you are claiming daily interest.

a Amount owing on promissory note: $8 000

b Interest at 18% per year to date of filing $ 760

c Daily interest from the date of filing
      Total: <u>$8 760</u>

(b) Claims over $10 000

As stated earlier, the most you can claim in Small Claims Court is $10 000 plus interest and expenses. But if you have a claim for more than that amount, you may be willing to lower your claim so you can take advantage of the Small Claims Court, rather than hire a lawyer to go to Supreme Court.

In that case, you must abandon part of your claim to bring it down to $10 000. Simply fill in the *How Much?* section, stating the full amount of each part of your claim and then add: "I abandon the amount of $_____" filling in the difference between the amount of your claim and $10 000. Then fill in the total of your claim, which will be $10 000 plus any interest you may be claiming.

a Amount owing on promissory note: $11 000

b Interest at 18% per year to date of filing $ 760

c Daily interest from the date of filing

I abandon the amount of $1 000

Total: $10 760

7. Signature

Don't forget to sign the Notice of Claim in the space provided.

b. FILING THE NOTICE OF CLAIM

Once you've filled out the Notice (see Sample #1) you must file it in the appropriate registry (See Appendix.)

"Filing" a document means giving it to the registry staff for entry in the court records. Normally, you will take it to the registry and give it to someone behind the counter who will check it over. Any errors he or she may notice can usually be fixed on the spot. If the Notice is accepted for filing — if everything is filled out properly — you will be asked to pay the filing fee. (At the time of writing, the fee is $25; however, fees change, so always check with the court registry first before filing.)

The fee must be paid by cash or by certified cheque or money order, payable to the Minister of Finance. Then the appropriate copies will be stamped and returned to you.

One copy is for your records. If you don't already have a file for this lawsuit, start one now and put your Notice of Claim at the front. You will see a registry file number has been entered in the upper right-hand corner of your Notice of Claim. Copy this number on the front of your file. You will want to refer to it any time you make an inquiry about your file at the registry.

Another copy is for the defendant. This is the one you will give to the defendant to let him or her know about the lawsuit. Be careful that you give the right copy. The defendant's copy has specific instructions to the defendant about what to do after receiving your Notice.

The service copy is the one you will attach to your Certificate of Service to prove that the defendant has been served with a copy of the Notice. (See chapter 3 for more about serving documents.)

If you cannot take the Notice of Claim personally to the registry, you may have someone file it for you or you may mail it in. However this will take some time particularly if the registry staff find an error and have to mail the form back to you before filing it. If you are using the mail, be sure you aren't going to run into a problem with time limits. (See section **a.5.** for more on this.)

c. SUMMARY

To begin an action in Small Claims Court, you must first complete the Notice of Claim. It is particularly important to be careful about naming the defendant. The claim should be described in your own words. After you have completed the Notice of Claim, you must file it in the appropriate court registry.

3
SERVING DOCUMENTS

a. WHAT DOES IT MEAN?

"Serving" a document simply means getting it to the person who is entitled to receive it, in whatever way the law requires.

The document to be served usually contains important information for the recipient — sometimes a warning that something must be done within a time limit. It is important that it be delivered in a way that ensures, as far as possible, that the person actually receives the document. It is also important to be able to prove that it was served properly and on time.

That's why the law has rules about how to serve documents. The rules for serving a Notice of Claim are contained in Rule 2 of the Small Claims Rules. The rules about serving all other documents are in Rule 18. A free copy of the Small Claims Rules is available from any Small Claims Court Registry.

b. PROCEDURE

After the Notice of Claim has been served, most other documents can be served by ordinary mail. The claimant's address will be on the Notice of Claim, and if the defendant files a Reply, his or her address will be on that. From then on it is up to each party to keep the others, and the court, informed of any change of address. Most documents that must be served can simply be mailed to the last address provided by the party.

When you use ordinary mail, the law assumes that the document has been served 14 days after the date you mailed it unless someone can prove otherwise.

c. SERVING THE NOTICE OF CLAIM

The Notice of Claim is just that: official notice that a claim is being made against the defendant. The law requires you to take special care to see that the defendant actually receives it. Unlike other documents that can simply be put in the ordinary mail, the Notice of Claim normally must either be delivered personally or be mailed by registered mail. As well, there are different kinds of defendants, and exactly how you must serve your Notice of Claim depends on what kind of defendant you have.

1. Personal service

Personal service means that you or someone acting on your behalf simply hands over the document to the defendant. If the person refuses to accept it, you may drop it on the table or floor in front of them.

Until recently, the claimant was not allowed to serve his or her own documents but that has now changed. However, whether for reasons of convenience or otherwise, you may not want to do the service yourself. You may have any adult person do it for you. This could be a friend who does it as a favor, or it could be a professional who charges a fee. These professionals are called "process servers" and they are listed under that heading in the Yellow Pages.

If you are using a process server, feel free to call several and ask them to quote their rates. Be sure to tell them that you are talking about Small Claims documents because they sometimes offer a better rate for those. When asking about fees, ask them to include the cost of completing the Certificate of Service. You may need this to prove the document has been served.

2. Registered mail

Registered mail is a simple and inexpensive way to serve a document. When you go to the post office to mail your document, be sure to ask for an "acknowledgment of receipt card." There is a small extra fee for this, but it means that you will receive a card back with the signature of the recipient. You can use this to prove that the document was in fact served, and the date of service.

3. Serving an individual

If your defendant is an individual person, you can serve your Notice of Claim personally or by registered mail. One disadvantage to using registered mail is that the person may refuse to accept the letter. You will have to wait to find that out and then try another method. In most cases, however, it is a quick and inexpensive method of service. Canada Post has an automated tracking system that allows you to check on the delivery status of your letter by calling a toll-free number without having to wait for the return of the acknowledgment of receipt card.

4. Serving a company

If your defendant is a company, you can send the Notice of Claim by registered mail to the company's registered office. Or, you may choose to leave it —

(a) at the registered office,

(b) at the company's place of business, with the person who seems to be in charge (e.g., a store manager),

(c) with a director or officer of the company, or

(d) if there is a liquidator or trustee in bankruptcy or receiver-manager, with that person.

If you did a company search before filling out your Notice of Claim, you will have the address of the registered office. Registered mail to that address is likely the simplest method and the easiest to prove.

5. Serving an out-of-province company

Companies from outside the province that operate in British Columbia should have someone who is appointed as the company's "attorney" in B.C. You can find out the name and address of this person from the Registrar of Companies in Victoria. If no such person has been appointed, you may use any of the methods listed above for serving a B.C. company.

6. Serving a partnership

You may serve a Notice of Claim on a partnership by registered mail to one of the partners or by leaving it —

(a) with a partner,

(b) at the partnership's place of business with the person who seems to be in charge (e.g., the manager), or

(c) with a receptionist.

7. Serving a defendant outside of British Columbia

If you are suing a defendant outside of the province, he or she is allowed more time to file a Reply. The Notice of Claim as printed says that the time limit for filing a Reply is 14 days. You must change this to 30 days on any Notice of Claim that is served outside of B.C.

d. WHAT IF THE USUAL METHODS DON'T WORK?

Sometimes you can't serve a document in the usual way because the person is determined not to be served. For example, he or she may refuse to come to the door or to accept a registered letter. Sometimes you don't know a person's exact address. You may know the community where the person lives but not have the street address or post office box number.

In that case, you must ask the registrar of the court to allow you to serve the Notice of Claim in some other way. To do that, fill out an Application to the Registrar (Form 16) and file it at the registry (see Sample #3). There is no charge for this, and the registrar may grant your order on the spot.

What you are asking for is called "substitutional service." That is, a method of service to substitute for the normal methods which haven't worked.

These are the usual methods of substitutional service:

(a) Posting the Notice on the defendant's door: Ask for this method when you know where the person lives but he or she refuses to answer the door.

(b) Leaving the Notice at his or her last known address: Consider this method if the person seems to have moved away but family or friends are still living at the person's old address.

(c) Sending the Notice by regular mail: Ask for this if the person has refused to accept a registered letter.

(d) Serving a relative of the defendant: A method to use if you don't know the person's address and can't find out.

(e) Advertising in a newspaper in the area where you believe the defendant now lives: This is expensive but it may be the only way if you don't have an address and can't show that some other method is likely to bring the Notice to the defendant's attention.

In your application, list all the attempts you have made to serve the Notice of Claim or to find the defendant's address. You may have used telephone and city directories, asked relatives, employers and friends, done searches at the motor vehicle registry, and even used a skip tracing agency. Then tell what method of service you would like to use and why you believe it is the most likely to succeed.

If you get an order for substitutional service, be sure to serve a copy of that order along with your Notice of Claim and the copy of the Reply form. The exception to this rule is

SAMPLE #3
APPLICATION TO THE REGISTRAR
(SUBSTITUTIONAL SERVICE)

APPLICATION TO THE REGISTRAR
IN THE PROVINCIAL COURT OF BRITISH COLUMBIA (SMALL CLAIMS COURT)

REGISTRY FILE NUMBER
13141516
REGISTRY LOCATION
Vancouver

FORM 16 (RULE 16)
SCL 216 (11-90)

Fill in the names of the parties, copying them from the Notice of Claim. Also, fill in the registry file number shown on the Notice of Claim.

In the case between:

Ruth Ryder   CLAIMANT(S)

and

Dennis Driver   DEFENDANT(S)

FROM:
Fill in the name, address and telephone number of the applicant.

NAME   Ruth Ryder
ADDRESS 57 Queen Street
                                                            555-3751
CITY, TOWN
MUNICIPALITY Kamloops   B.C.   V6N 3C7
                                    PROV   POSTAL CODE

Check the appropriate box.

The applicant asks for an order

- ☐ renewing a claim;
- ☐ postponing a settlement conference;
- ☐ extending the time for filing a certificate of readiness;
- ☒ permitting another method of service;
- ☐ permitting service of a notice of claim outside B.C.;
- ☐ exempting the applicant from paying fees;
- ☐ other:

Give the details of the order you are asking for.

I would like to be permitted to serve my Notice of Claim by
Regular Mail.

Give the facts you wish the registrar to consider and sign the Application.

The facts on which this application is based are as follows:
The Defendant has refused to accept service by registered mail.
I mailed the Notice of Claim to the defendant by registered mail
and the pink card was returned to me marked "Delivery refused."

I certify these facts are true.   *Ruth Ryder*
                                            SIGNATURE OF APPLICANT

This will be completed by the court.

The Court orders that

_____

_____

_____

_____

_____

    month   day   year   by the registrar

applicant copy

applicant copy

31

that if you are serving by advertisement, you do not have to include the order for substitutional service. Also, if your order for substitutional service includes a new time limit within which the defendant has to file a Reply to your Notice of Claim, cross out the time limit that is printed on the Notice of Claim and put in the new time limit.

e. WHEN MUST THE NOTICE OF CLAIM BE SERVED?

You have one year after you have filed your Notice of Claim to serve it on all the defendants. If the year is almost up and you are having trouble serving the defendants, go to the court registry at once and apply to renew your Notice of Claim. Even if the year has already gone by, you may be able to get a renewal, but it is much better to apply before the time is up.

f. PROVING THAT A DOCUMENT HAS BEEN SERVED

The service copy of the Notice of Claim has a Certificate of Service printed on the back (see Sample #4). If you have to prove that you served the Notice of Claim (if no Reply is filed), you will fill out the Certificate, stating:

(a) the name of the person who served it,

(b) the name of the person (or company, etc.) who was served,

(c) the date of service,

(d) the place of service, and

(e) the document that was served.

Then check off the method of service that was used. The person who served the Notice must sign the Certificate.

FORM 4A
SCL 004A (11-90)

CERTIFICATE OF SERVICE

I certify that

Fill in:
your name;

I   Robin Gardiner

the name of the party or
other person served;

Leslie Householder

served

the date service took
place with the address
or location.

on   October   29   199-   **at**   789 Main Street
         month   day   year   Prince George, B.C.

Tell what was served   **with**   a Notice of Claim (a copy of which is on the back of this certificate)

Tell how service took
place by checking
appropriate box(es) for: **by**

an individual;

   ✓ leaving a copy of it with him or her.

   ☐ mailing a copy of it by registered mail to him or her.

a company
incorporated under
the Company Act;

   ☐ mailing a copy of it by registered mail to the registered office of the company.

   ☐ leaving a copy of it   ☐ at the registered office of the company.

                ☐ at the place of business of the company, with a person who appears to manage or control the company's business there.

                ☐ with a director, officer, liquidator, trustee in bankruptcy or receiver manager of the company.

an extraprovincial
company;

   ☐ leaving a copy of it   ☐ with an attorney of the company appointed under section 328 of the Company Act.

                ☐ with a director, officer, liquidator, trustee in bankruptcy or receiver manager of the company.

a partnership;

   ☐ mailing a copy of it by registered mail to a partner.

   ☐ leaving a copy of it   ☐ with a partner.

                ☐ at the place of business of the partnership, with a person who appears to manage or control the partnership business there.

                ☐ with a receptionist who works at a place of business of the partnership.

November   5   199-   *Robin Gardiner*
month   day   year   signature of person who served the document.

g. SUMMARY

There are special rules about how parties to a lawsuit must get copies of documents to each other — that is, how they must *serve* the documents.

The rules for service of the Notice of Claim are more complicated than for most other documents. This is because this is the first official notice that the defendant has about the lawsuit and it's important that the right person receives it. Once the lawsuit is under way, everyone has provided their correct addresses and most documents can be served by ordinary mail.

4
IF YOU ARE BEING SUED

a. WHAT SHOULD THE DEFENDANT DO?

So far in this book, we have been talking about how to sue someone else. But you may be the one being sued. If so, you should read chapter 1 to get an idea of what Small Claims Court is about and to find out how to get more help if you need it. You should also at least have a quick look at chapters 2 and 3 to make sure that the claimant has done what is required.

However, the most important thing you will have to do when you receive a Notice of Claim is to decide how you are going to respond. Read the Notice carefully; you will probably come to one of the following conclusions:

- (a) You agree that you owe what is claimed and you want to pay it and be done with it.

- (b) You agree that you owe what is claimed but you just can't pay right now.

- (c) You agree that you owe the claimant something, but not as much as is claimed.

- (d) You agree that you owe the claimant something, but the claimant owes you something too.

- (e) Someone else should have to pay all or part of the claim.

- (f) You deny everything.

What to do in each of these cases is discussed below.

Note: You may be tempted to just ignore the whole thing, hoping it will go away. Chances are, it won't. If you do nothing, the claimant can get judgment against you without you even knowing about it. Then your bank account and pay cheque can be garnisheed, your goods can be seized, and you can be required to come to court to explain why you haven't paid (see chapter 13 for more about collection procedures). In almost every case, you will be better off if you respond in one of the following ways.

1. You agree with the claim and you want to pay

This one is easy, but maybe not as simple as it seems. If you pay the money directly to the claimant you will certainly want a receipt. Make sure that it says on it that it is "in full satisfaction of Small Claims action No. ____". Even so, the claim against you will still be on file at the court registry. You will want the claimant to sign a Notice of Withdrawal which you can file in the registry (see Sample #5). This will close the file so that the claimant cannot decide in future to go ahead with the suit, and nobody searching the court records will find an outstanding claim against you.

2. You owe the money but can't pay it right away

This is often the case. People usually want to pay their debts but sometimes circumstances make it impossible. Most claimants would rather work out an arrangement with you that will result in payment of the debt eventually, than go ahead with a lawsuit.

Depending on your relationship, you might try contacting the claimant directly and offering, for example, to sign a promissory note due on some date in the future when you feel you could pay. Or you might propose a schedule of regular payments. The court file could be left open until you make the promised payments, so that if you fail to pay, the claimant has the option of proceeding with the action.

SAMPLE #5
NOTICE OF WITHDRAWAL

NOTICE OF WITHDRAWAL

IN THE PROVINCIAL COURT OF BRITISH COLUMBIA (SMALL CLAIMS COURT)

IN THE CASE BETWEEN:

RUTH RYDER   **CLAIMANT(S)**

AND:

DENNIS DRIVER   **DEFENDANT(S)**

TAKE NOTICE that the _____Claimant_____ withdraws this

claim/~~counterclaim~~ against ____Dennis Driver____ .

May	16	199–
month	day	year

Ruth Ryder
signature

Name: ____Ruth Ryder____
print

Notice Served On:

Dennis Driver
Name of party

4567 Main Street
Address

Vancouver, B.C. V6C 2Z1

NOTIFYING OTHER PARTIES:

Rule 8(5) A party who withdraws a claim/counterclaim must promptly serve notice on all parties who were served with the claim/counterclaim and file a copy of the notice and proof of service with the Registry.

THE EFFECT OF WITHDRAWING:

RULE 8(6) A party who withdraws a claim/counterclaim may not at any time proceed with it or file another notice with respect to the claim/counterclaim without permission of a Judge. See Rule 16(7).

COURT DATE:

If a court date has been set for the claim/counterclaim it will be removed from the Court list once the Notice of Withdrawal has been filed.

If an agreement is not possible, or if you would rather not deal with the claimant directly, you must fill out the Reply that was served with the Notice of Claim and file it in the registry (see Sample #6). You will see on the form there is a space labelled REQUEST FOR PAYMENT SCHEDULE TO BE SET BY THE COURT. This is where you will put your proposal to pay the amount over time.

Try to make it a reasonable proposal. If it is, the claimant may accept it, or the court may order it anyway. If it is not reasonable and you can't be persuaded at the settlement conference (see chapter 7) to make a reasonable offer, the judge may refuse to order a payment schedule. In that case, the full amount would be due immediately.

Some examples of a proposal might be:

> I agree to pay $500. I could make the following payments: $300 on March 1, 199-, $100 on April 1, 199-, and $100 on May 1, 199-.

or

> I agree to pay $1 000. I could make the following payments: $100 on the 15th day of each month, from June 15, 199-, to March 1, 199-, inclusive.

or

> I agree to pay $300. I could make the following payments: $50 when the payment order is made and $250 on July 31, 199-.

Think about your proposal carefully. Try to make it one the claimant will accept but be sure it is one that you can manage.

SAMPLE #6
REPLY

REPLY

IN THE PROVINCIAL COURT OF BRITISH COLUMBIA (SMALL CLAIMS COURT)

FORM 2 (RULE 3)
SCL 002 (11 90)

REPLY

TO:
Copy the name, address and telephone number of the claimant from the Notice of Claim.

NAME Robin Gardiner
ADDRESS 123 King Street

CLAIMANT(S)

CITY, TOWN MUNICIPALITY Prince George   B.C. PROV   V6K 1L7 POSTAL CODE   TEL. 269-1234

FROM:
Fill in the name, address and telephone number of the defendant filing this reply.

NAME Leslie Householder
ADDRESS 789 Main Street

DEFENDANT

CITY, TOWN MUNICIPALITY Prince George   B.C. PROV   V6K 2M3 POSTAL CODE   TEL. 378-5678

DISPUTE:
Using the "HOW MUCH" section of the Notice of Claim as a guide, tell whether you agree or disagree with each part (a - e). If you disagree tell why.

a I told the Claimant in mid-June that I did not want my lawn cut anymore because the Claimant had destroyed two rosebushes.

b I agree that I owe $40.00 for two cuts.

c

d

e

REQUEST FOR PAYMENT SCHEDULE TO BE SET BY THE COURT

If you agree to pay all or part of what is claimed, make a proposal.

I agree to pay $ 40.00   GIVE DATES AND AMOUNTS   I could make the following payments:

$40.00 on January 15, 199-

If the claimant agrees with your proposal, you may file a consent order to end the lawsuit. Otherwise the registrar will set a date for a settlement conference and notify you.

COUNTERCLAIM   (YOU SHOULD ONLY FILL OUT THIS PART OF THE FORM IF YOU WISH TO MAKE A CLAIM AGAINST THE CLAIMANT)

WHAT HAPPENED?
Briefly tell what has led to your counterclaim.

The Claimant destroyed two prize rosebushes with a weed-eater and refused to replace them.

HOW MUCH?
Tell what you are claiming. If your counterclaim has more than one part, separate each part and fill in each individual amount, then add the individual amounts to make the total.

a Replacement cost of two rosebushes $ 50 00

b $

c $

TOTAL $ 50 00

Leslie Householder

SIGNATURE OF DEFENDANT

court copy

39

3. You do owe something, but not as much as is claimed

Maybe you agree, for example, that you do owe your contractor something for the work that was done, but the figure claimed is much too high.

Or maybe you admit that you did cause some damage to the claimant's property but he or she is asking you to pay as well for things that were not your fault.

You will use the DISPUTE section of the Reply to spell out exactly what you agree to and what you do not. Look at the HOW MUCH section of the Notice of Claim and decide what you will say about each item that was claimed. Use the lettered spaces in the Reply to respond to each item in the Notice of Claim. The following examples show how such a dispute might be written:

a The claimant says I owe $4 200 for electrical work. The claimant told me the work would cost about $3 000 and that is what I agreed to pay.

b I never agreed to pay interest and I deny that I owe this amount.

or

a The claimant claims for repair of damage that was done to her car before this accident. Only the right front door was involved.

b The claimant's clothes were not damaged in the accident.

c If the claimant missed five days' work it was not because of this accident.

The important thing is to respond specifically to each item that the claimant is asking for and tell what you do and do not agree with.

If the claim is for damages you are entitled to require the claimant to prove the amount.

40

4. You may owe the claimant something, but the claimant owes you something too

This might come about in two different ways. First, the claimant might owe you money from a prior debt, something unrelated to this case. Maybe she has an outstanding account with you for goods you supplied in the past and now she's suing you over other goods which she says are defective. In that case, you could claim the amount of the earlier unpaid invoice in your Reply to this claim.

Second, your claim might result from the same event that led to the claim against you. She might be claiming damages caused by what she says are defective goods: you deny the goods are defective and demand payment for them.

In the first case, your claim is technically called a "set-off." In the second case, it's a "counterclaim." However, in Small Claims Court, they are both dealt with as a counterclaim and you will see there is a space on the Reply form with that label (see Sample #6).

For instructions on how to fill out that section, see chapter 2, Getting Started, which tells how to fill out a Notice of Claim. The principles are the same. (See Sample #1 for a filled out copy of a Notice of Claim.)

Note that because the Counterclaim is a part of the Reply form, if you decide at some time *after* filing your Reply that you want to make a Counterclaim, you will have to file an amended Reply.

5. Someone else should have to pay all or part of the claim

Suppose you installed a skylight for a homeowner who is now suing you because the skylight is leaking and has caused damage. You don't know whether that's true or not but you feel that if it is, it is because the skylight itself was faulty. You think that the manufacturer should have to pay, if any one does.

If you think someone else should be liable for a claim that is being made against you, you should file a Third Party Notice (see Sample #7). This document adds the "third party" to the lawsuit. The third party then is in a position much like that of a defendant, in relation to your claim.

Because the Third Party Notice is very much like a Notice of Claim, you can get more information about how to fill out and file and serve the form in chapter 2, Getting Started. The Third Party Notice has to be served personally or by registered mail, the same as a Notice of Claim. See section **c.** in chapter 3 for more about serving the Notice of Claim.

6. You deny everything

It may be that you not only deny the amount that is claimed, but you deny that you are liable for anything at all. It may be that the claimant has sued the wrong person, or things didn't happen as he or she says, or it just didn't happen at all.

Use the DISPUTE section of the Reply form to deny each part of the claim that you dispute. If appropriate, you might make a general denial of everything:

> I dispute the amount of the claimant's claim and deny that I am liable to the claimant for any amount at all.

b. WHAT TO DO WITH YOUR REPLY

1. Fill out and file the Reply

Fill out the form, following all the instructions on the front page (fly sheet) and on the form itself (see Sample #6). You may use a typewriter or a ball point pen. Just be sure to print clearly and press hard enough so that all copies are readable. You may use a computer if you have software that allows you to fill out forms.

Then you must file it at the court registry. The address of the registry is in a box at the bottom of the Notice of Claim.

SAMPLE #7
THIRD PARTY NOTICE

FORM 3 (RULE 5)

THIRD PARTY NOTICE
IN THE PROVINCIAL COURT OF BRITISH COLUMBIA (SMALL CLAIMS COURT)

REGISTRY FILE NUMBER
9101112
REGISTRY LOCATION
Richmond

THIRD PARTY NOTICE

TO:
Fill in the name, address and telephone number of the person or business the defendant thinks should pay all or part of the claim against the defendant.

NAME ABC Skylites Ltd.
ADDRESS 690 1st Ave

THIRD PARTY

CITY TOWN MUNICIPALITY Burnaby   B.C. PROV   V6E 2B1 POSTAL CODE   TEL # 678-5544

FROM:
Fill in the name, address and telephone number of the defendant who is adding the third party.

NAME Robertsons Roofers Ltd.
ADDRESS 2020 E. 7th Ave

DEFENDANT

CITY TOWN MUNICIPALITY Richmond   B.C. PROV   V3I 2C4 POSTAL CODE   TEL # 378-1230

Copy the name, address and telephone number of the claimant from the notice of claim.

NAME Jordan Homeowner
ADDRESS 123 W. 4th Ave

CLAIMANT

CITY TOWN MUNICIPALITY Surrey   B.C. PROV   V2E 3B2 POSTAL CODE   TEL # 686-2166

WHAT HAPPENED?
Tell what happened to make you think the third party should pay all or part of the claim.

    I installed a skylight manufactured and supplied by the third party in a home owned by the Claimant. The Claimant says the roof has leaked. If so, I say it is because of a defective skylight.

HOW MUCH?
Tell what you are claiming from the third party. If the claim is made up of several parts, separate them here and show the amount for each part. Add these amounts and fill in the total claimed.

a	Cost of replacing skylight	$	950 00
b		$	
c		$	
d		$	
		$	
	TOTAL CLAIMED	$	950 00

SIGNATURE OF DEFENDANT

TIME LIMIT FOR THE THIRD PARTY
If the third party does not settle directly with the claimant and the defendant or file a reply **within 14 days**, a **court order may be made against** the third party. Then the third party will have to pay the amount claimed plus interest and further expenses.

The Court Address for filing documents is:

court copy

court copy

43

It's best to try to take it there in person. That way, the registry staff can look it over for you and let you know right away if there are any obvious problems with your form. If you have made a mistake, you can correct it right then.

If that's not possible, you can mail it, but be sure it will be received in time to meet the deadline. (See the section on time limits below.) You might want to use special mail to speed delivery or register your letter so you can prove the date of delivery. Of course you could have it delivered by courier or by someone else.

The registrar is also allowed to accept documents by fax. If you want to use this method, call your registry and ask if it will be accepted. If so, ask for the fax number.

2. Time limits

Look at the bottom of the Notice of Claim (Sample #1 in chapter 2) for the paragraph headed TIME LIMIT FOR A DEFENDANT. This will tell you when you must file your Reply. In most cases, it is 14 days from the day you receive the Notice. You don't count the day you received it and you don't count the day you file the Reply.

Suppose you were served with the Notice of Claim on the 10th of the month. You have 14 days to file your Reply, not counting the day of service or the day of filing. Therefore, you must file your Reply no later than the 25th.

If you were served outside of British Columbia, however, or if there were other unusual circumstances, you may have longer than the usual 14 days. If so, that should be written in on the Notice of Claim. If the claimant got an order for substitutional service on you (that is, to serve you in other than the ordinary way), you should also be given a copy of the court order allowing that method of service. That court order should contain a statement of the number of days you have to file your Reply, and the same time limit should appear on your Notice of Claim.

3. If you miss the deadline

If you don't file your Reply in the time allowed, the claimant can ask the court for a default order. This is an order made against you, in your absence. If the claim is for a specified amount, the order will likely be for the full amount claimed. If it is for damages, a date will be set for a hearing. At that time the claimant will appear before a judge and prove the amount of the damages that he or she is entitled to. You will not get a notice of when that hearing is.

If you have missed the deadline but still want to file a Reply, you may still have a chance to do so.

If the claim was for a specified amount, contact the registry and find out whether a default order has been granted. If not, go ahead and file your Reply right away.

If the claim was for damages, find out whether a date has been set for the hearing. If not, you may still file your Reply. If a date has been set, you will first have to apply to the court for permission to file your Reply. (See chapter 8, Applications to Court.)

To find out what to do if a default order has been made against you, see chapter 5, If No Reply is Filed.

4. Serving the other parties

The registry takes care of serving any other parties for you. Within 21 days after you file your Reply, the registry must serve a copy on all other parties. They normally do this by mail or by giving a copy to a claimant who comes into the registry.

c. SUMMARY

If a defendant who receives a Notice of Claim admits the claim, there is no need for a trial. A defendant who needs time to pay may use the Reply to say so and to propose a payment schedule. The claimant may accept the proposal, or there can be a payment hearing, with a judge making the payment order. A defendant who disputes a claim will complete the Reply, including the reasons for the dispute. The Reply must be filed with the court within the time allowed. Then the court staff will see that the other parties receive a copy.

5
IF NO REPLY IS FILED

a. IN AN ACTION FOR A SPECIFIED AMOUNT

If you are claiming a specified amount — an amount owing on an invoice or a promissory note, for example — then after the time allowed for filing the Reply is expired, you can ask for a Default Order. A Default Order is an order of the court with the same force as if the order were made, for example, after a trial. The claimant can use it to garnishee a bank account or pay cheque or to seize the defendant's goods. (Rule 6 of the Small Claims Rules deals with Default Orders and what happens when no Reply is filed.)

To ask for a Default Order, you must complete an Application for Default Order (see Sample #8). It is a simple form to fill out and the bottom half contains the Default Order itself.

Simply fill in the names of the parties, check the box indicating that no hearing is required, and fill in the amounts as claimed in the Notice of Claim. The expenses may include any costs incurred to serve the Notice of Claim, even if the amount is different from what was in the Notice of Claim. Check with the registrar if there are questions about this amount.

You must then file this application form, *together with* the Certificate of Service, at the court registry. (The Certificate of Service is required to prove that the defendant actually received the Notice of Claim, so be sure that it is filled out fully and accurately.)

SAMPLE #8
APPLICATION FOR DEFAULT ORDER

APPLICATION FOR DEFAULT ORDER
IN THE PROVINCIAL COURT OF BRITISH COLUMBIA (SMALL CLAIMS COURT)

FORM 5 (RULE 6)
SCE 005-111 90

REGISTRY FILE NUMBER
45678
REGISTRY LOCATION
Prince George

APPLICATION FOR DEFAULT ORDER

Fill in the names, copying them from the notice of claim.

In the case between:
ROBIN GARDINER   CLAIMANT(S)

and

LESLIE HOUSEHOLDER   DEFENDANT(S)

The registry staff will fill in this section.

X . No hearing is required as the claim is for a debt.

or

A hearing is required before a Judge of the Provincial Court, because the claim is not for a debt. At the hearing, the Judge will determine the amount the claimant is entitled to, or the terms of an appropriate order for this case.

A HEARING WILL BE HELD ON

month   day   year   at   time   M   or as soon after this time as the court schedule allows.

at

court location

If you cannot attend this hearing please notify the Court Registry.
If you do not attend at the time set for the default hearing, the Judge may cancel it.

Fill in this section.

DEFAULT ORDER

If you appeared in court the judge will have told you what the terms of the order are.

It no court appearance was required, the terms of the order will be those requested on your Notice of Claim.

As Leslie Householder
          defendant
has not filed a reply and the claimant has proved the defendant has been served with the notice of claim, **THIS COURT ORDERS THE DEFENDANT TO:**

PAY DIRECTLY TO THE CLAIMANT THE SUM OF	$	240 00	amount of claim granted by court
	+ $	35 00	expenses
	+ $	6 00	interest
	= $	281 00	TOTAL AMOUNT

This will be signed and dated by the court

month   day   year   by the court

THE DEFENDANT IS ORDERED TO CARRY OUT THE TERMS OF THE ORDER IMMEDIATELY.

court copy

48

If you file the Application for Default Order and Certificate of Service, properly completed, the registrar must sign the Default Order.

b. IN AN ACTION FOR DAMAGES

If the claim is for damages, you must appear before a judge to prove the amount of the damages before being entitled to a Default Order. In this case, you must complete the Application for Default Order and check the second box indicating that a hearing is required. Registry staff will fill in the date and time of the hearing. If you have a problem with the date, speak to someone at the registry and ask him or her to change it. This form then becomes your reminder of the date and time of your hearing.

Come to the hearing prepared to present evidence of the amount of your damages. This evidence might include invoices for repair work, pay slips showing loss of wages, and so on. Remember that if the defendant has not filed a Reply, you do not have to prove that the defendant is *liable* (responsible) for the damages; it's only the *amount* of the damages that must be proven. Also, the defendant has no right to take part in this hearing and will not be notified about it.

After your hearing, registry staff will fill in the amounts you are entitled to, and sign the Default Order. (For more about preparing for this hearing, see chapter 8.)

c. CAN A DEFAULT ORDER BE CANCELLED?

Like any other order that is made in the absence of one of the parties, a Default Order can, in some cases, be cancelled (set aside). (Rule 17(1) of the Small Claims Court Rules deals with cancelling orders.) The defendant against whom the order is made must apply to the court within a reasonable time and must show a good reason for cancelling the order.

For example, suppose a claimant serves a Notice of Claim on a business by leaving the Notice with a receptionist who never passes it on to anyone in authority. The boss doesn't find out about it until after a Default Order is obtained and the company's bank account is garnished. The defendant applies to the court immediately to cancel the Default Order, saying there is a good defence to the claim and he or she didn't know about the lawsuit until now.

An application to cancel a Default Order involves three steps:

(a) Fill out the form (see Sample #9).

(b) Serve it.

(c) Appear in court.

The important points the court will consider when deciding whether to cancel a Default Judgment are —

(a) Did the defendant act promptly once he or she learned about the Default Judgment?

(b) Was there a valid reason for not filing a Reply in time?

(c) Is there a reasonable defence to the claim?

To make an application to cancel a Default Order, a defendant must complete the Application to a Judge and file it with the Small Claims registry (see Sample #9). There is no charge for this.

Then the defendant must serve a copy of the application on every party who will be affected by it (usually just the claimant) at least seven days before the date set for the hearing. If you are going to use ordinary mail to serve this notice, remember that you must allow fourteen days from the date of mailing (that's when it is presumed to be served) plus the seven-day notice period. So be sure to allow enough time when you set the date for the hearing.

At the hearing, the defendant will make his or her argument to the judge about why the Default Order should be cancelled and the claimant will have the opportunity to say

APPLICATION TO A JUDGE

IN THE PROVINCIAL COURT OF BRITISH COLUMBIA (SMALL CLAIMS COURT)

FORM 17 (RULE 16)
SCL 017 (1190)

REGISTRY FILE NUMBER
45678
REGISTRY LOCATION
Prince George

APPLICATION TO A JUDGE

Fill in the names of the parties, copying them from the Notice of Claim. Also, fill in the registry file number shown on the Notice of Claim.

In the case between:

ROBIN GARDINER — CLAIMANT(S)

and

LESLIE HOUSEHOLDER — DEFENDANT(S)

FROM:
Fill in the name, address and telephone number of the applicant.

NAME / ADDRESS: Leslie Householder
789 Main Street

CITY, TOWN, MUNICIPALITY: Prince George   PROV: B.C.   POSTAL CODE: V6K 2M3   TEL: 378-5678

APPLICANT

The registry staff will tell you the date of the hearing.

An application will be made to the court

on December 15 199- at 10 A M or as soon after this time as the court schedule allows.

at 1600 3rd Ave, Prince George

Give details of the order you are asking for.

for the following order:

An order cancelling the Default Order which was made in this case on November 15, 199-.

Give the facts you wish the court to consider and then sign the Application.

The facts on which the application is based are as follows:

On the day after I was served with the Notice of Claim I was in a car accident and was hospitalized for three weeks. I telephoned the Claimant and said that I intended to dispute the Claim.

I certify these facts are true.   *Leslie Householder*
SIGNATURE OF APPLICANT

This will be completed by the court.

The Court orders that

_____
_____
_____
_____

month   day   year   by the Court

court copy

court copy

why it should not be. The defendant who is asking for this cancellation must be very careful to follow the rules precisely because the court will not be anxious to set aside an Order that was properly obtained, unless a very clear case is made.

If the judge agrees to cancel the Order, the defendant will fill out the cancellation Order and file it in the registry. Then the defendant must fill out and file the Reply. (This can be done at the same time.)

d. SUMMARY

A defendant has a certain amount of time to file a Reply to a Notice of Claim. Normally, it is 14 days after receiving the Notice. If no Reply is filed in that time, the claimant can ask the court for an Order granting the claim. As long as the claimant can prove that the defendant was properly served with the Notice of Claim, the Order will be granted. If the claim was for a certain amount of money, the court will order the defendant to pay that amount to the claimant. If it was for an unspecified amount of damages, there will be a hearing at which the claimant will have to prove the amount. If a defendant has a good reason for being late with the Reply, it may be possible to get a court order allowing it to be filed even after the deadline is past.

6

IF A REPLY IS FILED

a. THE REGISTRY MUST NOTIFY OTHER PARTIES

Within 21 days after a Reply is filed, the registry must serve copies on all other parties. Normally this will be done by mail, but if you are the claimant, you can go to the registry and pick up a copy if you wish.

Everyone will also be sent a Notice of Settlement Conference (see Sample #10). **Note:** It is most important that you go to the settlement conference; if it turns out that the date you are given is impossible for you, contact the registry immediately.

b. IF THE CLAIM IS FOR PERSONAL INJURIES

1. Certificate of readiness

If your claim is for damages as a result of personal injuries (e.g., in a car accident), you must file a Certificate of Readiness before a date will be set for a settlement conference (see Sample #11). This is because personal injury cases usually cannot be settled until all the relevant medical reports are in, as well as records of lost earnings, and other expenses, both past and projected.

You have six months to file this certificate of readiness, together with copies of all medical reports and records of expenses and losses both past and expected. If for any reason it cannot be filed in that time, you must ask the registrar to extend the time limit.

SAMPLE #10
NOTICE OF SETTLEMENT CONFERENCE

NOTICE OF SETTLEMENT CONFERENCE

NOTICE OF SETTLEMENT CONFERENCE
IN THE PROVINCIAL COURT OF BRITISH COLUMBIA (SMALL CLAIMS COURT)

FORM 6 (RULE 7)
SCL 006 (11-90)

REGISTRY FILE NUMBER
45678
REGISTRY LOCATION
Prince George

In the case between:
ROBIN GARDINER

CLAIMANT(S)

and

LESLIE HOUSEHOLDER

DEFENDANT(S)

A settlement conference will be held on

| January | 5 | 199– | at | 10 | A M | or as soon after this time as the court schedule allows. |
| month | day | year | | | | |

at   1600 3rd Ave, Prince George
court location

Who must attend?
All parties must attend the settlement conference, either with or without their representatives.

A party who is not an individual (for example a corporation or a partnership) must be represented by someone who has authority to settle the claim.

What is the purpose of the settlement conference?
There are two main purposes for the settlement conference
(a)   to encourage settlement of cases; and
(b)   if settlement is not possible, to help the parties prepare their cases for trial.

What happens if someone does not attend?
The judge may make a payment order or other appropriate order against a party who does not attend a settlement conference.

Note:
For more information there is a booklet called "Getting Ready for Court"

| December | 18 | 199– | J. M. Registrar |
| month | day | year | by the court |

court copy

court copy

54

SAMPLE #11
CERTIFICATE OF READINESS

FORM 7 (RULE 7)
SCL 007 (11/90)

CERTIFICATE OF READINESS
IN THE PROVINCIAL COURT OF BRITISH COLUMBIA (SMALL CLAIMS COURT)

REGISTRY FILE NUMBER
13141516
REGISTRY LOCATION
Vancouver

Fill in the names of the parties, copying them from the notice of claim. Also, fill in the registry file number shown on the notice of claim.

In the case between:

RUTH RYDER   CLAIMANT(S)

and

DENNIS DRIVER   DEFENDANT(S)

FROM:
Fill in the name, address and telephone number of the claimant who is filing the certificate.

NAME   Ruth Ryder   CLAIMANT
ADDRESS   57 Queen Street

CITY TOWN
MUNICIPALITY Kamloops   B.C.   V6N 3C7   TEL # 375-1234
              PROV.   POSTAL CODE

I am claiming damages for personal injuries and am ready to discuss settlement of my entire claim with a judge at a settlement conference.

I attach all medical reports and all records of expenses or losses incurred or expected.

Fill in the date and sign here.

June   4   199-   *Ruth Ryder*
month   day   year   signature of claimant

court copy

court copy

55

Once the certificate is filed, you have 14 days to serve the other parties with a copy of the certificate along with copies of all attached reports and records. Remember that if you use ordinary mail, the documents are considered to be received 14 days after you mail them, so you should be ready to mail your copies out the same day you file with the court.

2. Medical examination of the claimant

In a personal injury case, the defendant may want to have another medical opinion about the extent and nature of the claimant's injuries. In that case, the defendant can apply to a judge for an order that the claimant must be examined by a doctor. The defendant may choose the doctor but also must pay for the examination.

The doctor will give a written report to the defendant. The defendant must then serve a copy of the report on the claimant at least seven days before the settlement conference and must also bring a copy of the report to the settlement conference.

3. Settlement conference on liability

Cases involving personal injuries caused in motor vehicle accidents often involve two separate issues:

(a) Who is "liable" (legally responsible) for the accident?

(b) What is the extent of the damages?

It can take quite a lot of time and expense preparing the medical and other evidence required to prove the extent of the damages. It also can take a lot of work on the defendant's part to prepare to dispute that evidence. If the claimant fails to prove that the defendant is liable for the injuries, all of that preparation will have been wasted.

Therefore, either party in a personal injury case can ask for a settlement conference on the issue of liability only. This is almost always a good idea if there is any doubt at all about liability.

c. SUMMARY

After the defendant files a Reply, the court registry will send copies to the other parties. They also will set a date for a settlement conference and send notices to everyone.

If it's a personal injury case, a settlement conference will not be scheduled until the claimant files a Certificate of Readiness. This must be done within six months of filing the Notice of Claim unless an extension is granted. The defendant may ask for a court order requiring the claimant to be examined by a doctor of the defendant's choice. Either side can ask for a settlement conference on the issue of liability only.

7
THE SETTLEMENT CONFERENCE

a. WHAT IS IT?

The settlement conference is your opportunity to sit down with the other side in your case, and with a judge, and try to resolve the problem. This is something new in Small Claims Court and it has been proving very effective. In Vancouver, two-thirds of all cases are settled during or after the settlement conference and never need to go to trial. Throughout the province, the average is 60%.

After the defendant has filed a Reply, all the parties to the case will receive a Notice of Settlement Conference in the mail (see Sample #10 in chapter 6). These conferences are set for a specific date and time. Different court locations use different scheduling practices, but most courts schedule the conferences for about one-half hour each.

The conference is held in an office or boardroom or any other similar type of room that might be available — not in a courtroom. You will sit around a table with the judge. The atmosphere is less formal than in the courtroom. It's very much a case of "Let's get down to business and see if we can't agree on a resolution." (The rules about settlement conferences are found in Rule 7 of the Small Claims Court Rules.)

b. HOW TO PREPARE

Read chapter 9 on Preparing for Trial. If you are smart, you will do all your trial preparation *before the settlement conference.* That way you will be able to tell the judge very clearly and briefly exactly what your case is about. And, maybe more important, you will be able to tell how you will be able to prove that case.

You will be expected to have with you all the documents, letters and so on that you need to support your case. If you have done your trial preparation, your documents will all be available and in order. In fact, if you don't have your documents that are essential to the case with you, the judge might order everyone to come back on another day to complete the conference and could require you to pay the other side's expenses of coming back.

Don't forget that not a lot of time is available for most settlement conferences, so you will be at an advantage if you are prepared to say what you need to and to show the judge the documents you want to be considered. Don't waste valuable time fumbling through papers looking for your mechanic's estimate or trying to put your thoughts in order.

What's more, if you get to trial and try to use as evidence a document that you did *not* bring to the settlement conference, the judge could refuse to allow it. Or, again, the judge could adjourn the trial to allow the other side some time to deal with your new evidence and require you to pay the extra expenses of coming back on another day.

If there is a document you know you will need but you just can't get hold of it in time for the settlement conference, it is up to you to have the conference postponed until you do have the document. For example, you might be waiting for a medical report or a repair estimate that is taking longer than you expected.

You must apply for an order postponing the settlement conference and you must do this at least seven days before the date for the conference. This is another reason to do your preparation well in advance of the date; then you will know what it is you have and what you still need in the way of documentation. When asking for a postponement, it is easiest if you have talked to the other side and can let the court registry know when you would both be prepared to go ahead with the conference.

To apply for a postponement of the settlement conference, you must complete an Application to the Registrar, which is the same form shown as Sample #3 in chapter 3 and as Sample #12 in chapter 8. In this case, you would check off the box beside "postponing a settlement conference."

c. WHO MUST ATTEND?

The parties themselves all are expected to attend, that is, the claimant(s) and the defendant(s). Some judges will allow a lawyer to attend on behalf of a client in some cases, but most prefer to deal with clients directly because the object is to settle the case. Lawyers usually aren't in a position to agree to a settlement on the spot. However, if you have a good reason to want to send a lawyer to a settlement conference on your behalf, contact the court registry. You may need to make an application to a judge.

When the party is a company or partnership, the person representing the party at the settlement conference must be someone who has authority to settle the claim. Usually this would be an officer of the company or a partner.

An order can be made against any party who fails to attend a settlement conference. If you are the claimant, this means your claim can be dismissed if you don't show up. If you are the defendant, a payment order can be made against you. If so, the whole amount of the claim would be due immediately.

If this happens to you by accident, whether you forgot the date or were unable to attend for some reason, contact the registry immediately.

d. TELEPHONE CONFERENCES

In some cases a judge may agree to hold a settlement conference over the telephone. Telephone conferences may be used if one party is so far away from the court that it would be a hardship to attend. Contact your court registry for details if you would like a telephone conference.

e. THE JUDGE

The judge who hears the settlement conference will *not* be the judge who hears your trial if you end up having one. This means that you can be very candid in discussing your position at the settlement conference without worrying about prejudicing your case later.

The judge will ask questions and encourage you to tell what result you need and can live with. Be prepared to present a realistic settlement proposal.

f. WHAT RESULT CAN YOU EXPECT?

1. Settlement

As stated earlier, the main purpose of the settlement conference is to settle the case, and in many instances, that is what happens. After each person tells his or her story, with the judge perhaps asking some questions, the parties agree on a solution. If that happens, then the judge will make an order in the terms that the parties agree to.

Often it's a matter of working out a payment schedule that both sides can live with. If you are the defendant and you feel that you do owe at least some of the money that is claimed but you can't pay it at once, bring along pay slips and any other evidence you have of your financial situation. Then be prepared to propose an instalment plan that is both realistic from your point of view and fair to the claimant.

If the judge does order a payment schedule, even though it is agreed to by both sides, be sure that the order is properly filed with the court so that it is on the record. That way, as long as you make the payments required by the Order, the claimant cannot take any enforcement steps against you. If you are the claimant, by having the Order entered on the record, you are in a position to enforce it if the defendant fails to meet its terms. (See chapter 11 for more on payment orders.)

2. Partial settlement

Sometimes only part of a case can be settled. For example, in a claim arising out of a car accident, the defendant may have no trouble agreeing that the cost of repairing the car is just as the claimant says. But the defendant may disagree entirely that he or she was responsible for the accident. In that case, the judge could set the damages in the amount that the parties agree on. Then at the trial, the claimant only has to prove that the defendant was liable (responsible) for the accident. The claimant won't have to bring photos of the damage to the car or repair estimates, invoices, and so on.

Even where the parties don't agree, the judge can decide some issues that don't require any evidence. For example, suppose a homeowner sues a contractor for failing to live up to the terms of a building contract. The contractor denies liability because it was an employee who did the substandard work, and the employee has already been fired. The judge could decide at the settlement conference that the contractor is responsible for the actions of his or her employee. Then at the trial, it would be up to the homeowner to prove what happened.

3. Planning for a trial

If a complete settlement cannot be achieved, the settlement conference gives a good opportunity to do some things that will help the trial go more smoothly and quickly.

First, the settlement conference is where the trial date will be set. Be sure to be aware of your schedule, holiday plans, and so on when you come to the settlement conference because it is much easier to set a date when everyone is together with their calendars than to try to change it later.

The judge will not tell you at the settlement conference how to present your case at trial, but if you have specific questions about what evidence you will need, for example, you certainly may ask those questions at that time.

You can also ask the judge to order the other side to do certain things. For example, you can ask that the other side be required to produce certain evidence at trial. Or the other side may have certain documents that you want to look at. It may be that they are very lengthy and you just want a chance to look through them to see if there is anything helpful. The judge can order the other side to make certain documents available for you to look at and to copy, where appropriate.

If you are the defendant and there is a claim for damage to property, such as damage caused to a car in an accident, you may want to have your own mechanic have a look at it. You might want your mechanic to give evidence about the cost of repair or you may simply want some help in preparing the questions you will ask of the claimant's mechanic.

The judge has quite a lot of power to deal with matters at the settlement conference. In fact, he or she may make any order "for the just, speedy, and inexpensive resolution of the claim." If there is something you want but you aren't sure how or if it can be done, ask the judge.

g. SUMMARY

The settlement conference is an opportunity for the parties to get together, with a judge, and try to settle the case. If the case can't be settled, at least some points might be agreed upon and some questions answered. The parties should be well prepared to summarize their case to the judge and to describe the evidence that will be used at trial if necessary. All documents should be brought to the conference. There are a number of orders the judge can make at the conference. If a trial is still needed, the trial date will be set at the conclusion of the settlement conference.

8
APPLICATIONS TO COURT

There are a number of reasons why you might need to make an application to the court before or after a small claims trial. (The rules about applications are found in Rule 16 of the Small Claims Rules.)

a. TYPES OF APPLICATIONS

1. Applications to a judge

Some applications require a hearing before a judge. Examples are applications —

    (a) To postpone a trial

    (b) For a default order in respect of a counterclaim

    (c) To file a reply after the time limit

    (d) For a medical examination of a party

    (e) Setting another place for trial

    (f) Cancelling a summons to a witness

    (g) For a payment hearing despite an outstanding writ of seizure and sale

    (h) To change or cancel an order made in the absence of a party

    (i) To change or cancel the terms of a payment schedule

    (j) To extend or shorten a time limit

    (k) For an order against a party who fails to obey a rule

    (l) To review a decision of a registrar

2. Applications to a registrar

Other applications require no hearing and can be granted by a registrar of the court. Examples of those that do not require a hearing are applications —

(a) To renew a claim after time for service has run out

(b) To postpone a settlement conference

(c) To extend the time for filing a certificate of readiness in a personal injury case

(d) To allow service of a Notice of Claim outside B.C. where the rules don't otherwise allow

(e) To allow an alternative method of service (substituted service)

(f) For an exemption from filing fees

3. Applications by consent

Often, both sides can agree on these applications. If so, the registrar can make the order, without any hearing, regardless of what the application is for. One party simply needs to fill out an application form and satisfy the registrar that the other side agrees. Usually a letter signed by the other party will be required.

b. HOW TO APPLY

Whether the application is to a judge or to a registrar, the person making it must fill out the appropriate application form and file it (see Samples #12 and #13). The form for an application to a registrar lists the usual types of applications and asks you to check off the one that applies. The form for an application to a judge asks you to write in the order being sought.

In either case, you will also be asked to fill in the facts on which the application is based. Use your own words and make it brief.

I am applying for an order postponing the settlement conference which is scheduled for June 19, 199-, until the week of July 7.

I need a report from Dr. Leslie Wong. Dr. Wong has been on vacation for the past month and has promised to provide a report by June 20, 199-.

Sometimes a person wants to file an application in a registry other than where the file is. This will be allowed if all parties agree or if the registrar is satisfied that the application is urgent.

c. SERVING THE OTHER PARTIES

If the application is one that requires a hearing (i.e., an Application to a Judge), it must be served on any other person who could be affected by it. The two exceptions to this rule are —

(a) an application that the registrar is satisfied is urgent, and

(b) an application for a default order in respect of a counterclaim or third party notice. (The other party has failed to file a reply and so is not entitled to notice of the hearing.)

If the application is one that does not require a hearing, then nothing needs to be served on anyone else.

Of course once you get the order in response to the application, you must serve it on anyone who is affected by it.

d. THE HEARING

If a hearing is required, the registrar will give you a date and time to appear. The other side may appear and be heard as well. If you are unable to attend, you should contact the registry and ask to be heard by telephone conference.

SAMPLE #12
APPLICATION TO THE REGISTRAR

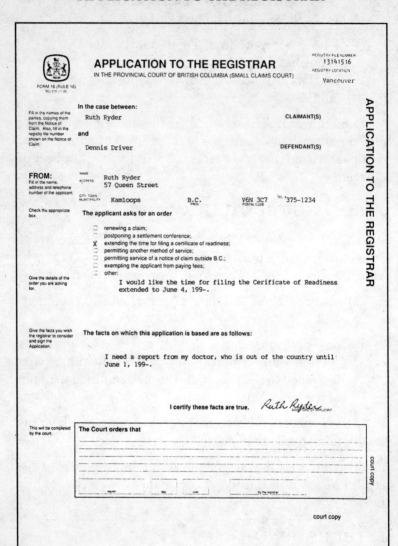

APPLICATION TO THE REGISTRAR
IN THE PROVINCIAL COURT OF BRITISH COLUMBIA (SMALL CLAIMS COURT)

FORM 16 (RULE 16)
SCL 016 (11 95)

REGISTRY FILE NUMBER
13141516
REGISTRY LOCATION
Vancouver

Fill in the names of the parties, copying them from the Notice of Claim. Also, fill in the registry file number shown on the Notice of Claim.

In the case between:

Ruth Ryder   CLAIMANT(S)

and

Dennis Driver   DEFENDANT(S)

FROM:
Fill in the name, address and telephone number of the applicant.

NAME / ADDRESS
Ruth Ryder
57 Queen Street

CITY / TOWN / MUNICIPALITY   Kamloops   B.C. PROV   V6N 3C7 POSTAL CODE   TEL. 375-1234

Check the appropriate box.

The applicant asks for an order

☐ renewing a claim;
☐ postponing a settlement conference;
☒ extending the time for filing a certificate of readiness;
☐ permitting another method of service;
☐ permitting service of a notice of claim outside B.C.;
☐ exempting the applicant from paying fees;
☐ other:

Give the details of the order you are asking for.

I would like the time for filing the Cerificate of Readiness extended to June 4, 199-.

Give the facts you wish the registrar to consider and sign the Application.

The facts on which this application is based are as follows:

I need a report from my doctor, who is out of the country until June 1, 199-.

I certify these facts are true.   *Ruth Ryder*
SIGNATURE OF APPLICANT

This will be completed by the court.

The Court orders that

_____
_____
_____
_____

month   day   year   By the registrar

court copy

court copy

68

SAMPLE #13
APPLICATION TO A JUDGE

APPLICATION TO A JUDGE
IN THE PROVINCIAL COURT OF BRITISH COLUMBIA (SMALL CLAIMS COURT)

REGISTRY FILE NUMBER
45678
REGISTRY LOCATION
Prince George

FORM 17 (RULE 16)
SCL 017 (11/90)

Fill in the names of the parties, copying them from the Notice of Claim. Also, fill in the registry file number shown on the Notice of Claim.

In the case between:

Robin Gardiner

CLAIMANT(S)

and

Leslie Householder

DEFENDANT(S)

FROM:
Fill in the name, address and telephone number of the applicant.

NAME   Leslie Householder
ADDRESS 789 Main Street

APPLICANT

CITY, TOWN,
MUNICIPALITY Prince George   B.C.   V6K 2M3   TEL. 378-5678
                              PROV.   POSTAL CODE

The registry staff will tell you the date of the hearing.

An application will be made to the court

on | December | 15 | 199- | at | 10 | A.M | or as soon after this time as the court schedule allows.
     month   day   year   time

at | 1600 3rd Ave, Prince George |
                court location

Give details of the order you are asking for.

for the following order:

An order allowing a late Reply to be filed.

Give the facts you wish the court to consider and then sign the Application.

The facts on which the application is based are as follows:

On the day after I was served with the Notice of Claim I was in a car accident and was hospitalized for three weeks. I telephoned the Claimant and said that I intended to dispute the claim.

I certify these facts are true.   *Leslie Householder*
                                  SIGNATURE OF APPLICANT

This will be completed by the court.

The Court orders that

month	day	year	by the Court

court copy

court copy

69

Be prepared to explain the background and reasons for your application and to tell the judge exactly what you want. If you have any documents to support your evidence, be sure to bring them with you.

e. SUMMARY

Some kinds of orders can be granted by a registrar on the basis of a written application by one party. These do not need to be served on the other parties. Other orders, more contentious matters generally, require a hearing before a judge. The party applying fills out a form, serves it on the other parties, and then must appear before a judge to argue in favor of the application. The other side can appear at the same time to dispute it, or can send a letter.

Any application that is agreed to by all the affected parties can be made by a registrar without a hearing.

9
PREPARING FOR TRIAL

a. CHANGING THE DATE

If for some reason you need to change the trial date, the easiest way is to get the other parties to agree. If they do agree, you can write a letter to the court registry saying that all parties agree to an adjournment, and asking for a new trial date (see Sample #14). However, note that adjournments are rarely granted, even when the parties agree, unless application is made at least one month before the trial.

You should first telephone the registry and find out when a trial date would be available and, according to what you are told, ask in your letter for a trial on that date, or during the time suggested: "during the week of February 10," for example.

If the other side refuses to agree, you will have to ask the judge to adjourn the trial. You can do this by making an application in advance of the trial date (see chapter 8, Applications to Court) or you can show up on the date set for the trial and ask that it be adjourned. If you do this, you will be more likely to get your adjournment if you have a very good reason and have notified the other side in advance that you intend to ask for the delay. If you haven't notified the other side, you will likely have to pay their witness costs, if any.

SAMPLE #14
LETTER REQUESTING NEW TRIAL DATE

Leslie Householder
789 Main Street
Prince George, B.C.
V6K 2M3
378-5678

Small Claims Court Registry
1600 Third Avenue
Prince George
V2L 3G6

January 7, 199-

To the Registrar:

Re: Case No. 45678, January 20, 199-

We spoke today and I told you that all parties have agreed to adjourn this trial. You told me the date of January 28, 199- is available and we all agree to hold the trial on this date.

Yours truly,

Leslie Householder

Leslie Householder

Keep in mind that the courts are reluctant to grant adjournments because they want to keep court time on schedule.

b. CHANGING YOUR DOCUMENTS

Sometimes when you are getting ready to present your case, you will find that you want to change something or add something to your Notice of Claim or your Reply.

If you haven't had your settlement conference yet, it's very simple to change a document. If it's a Notice of Claim, for example, get a new form from the registry. Fill it out the like the old one, making your changes. Underline every change (in red if you can), and put your initials and the date next to each change.

Then file the changed document in the registry and serve copies on the other parties. (Even though this is a Notice of Claim it can be served by ordinary mail like any other document because you already have everyone's address for service.)

Often the need for a change in a document comes up during the settlement conference. If the settlement conference has already begun, you need a judge's permission to make a change, but this can be done right at the conference.

If you find that you need to make a change *after* the conference has taken place, you must make an application to a judge for permission (see chapter 8). If it's a major change, you might instead ask the registry to schedule another settlement conference where you could ask permission to make the change and also possibly settle the claim. The other possibility is to wait until trial day and make a "preliminary application" for your change. This procedure is discussed in section **d.** of chapter 10.

c. IF YOU ARE THE CLAIMANT

1. Getting ready

If this is your first small claims case, you might begin your preparation for court by reading chapter 10 to find out what will happen at the trial. (Rule 10 of the Small Claims Rules deals with the trial itself.) If possible, you might also attend a few Small Claims Court trials, as an observer. All trials are open to the public and you are free to enter and leave the courtroom at any time. Remember that each case is different and judges have their own individual styles, but if you watch a few cases you should have some idea of what to expect when it's your turn.

2. Making a trial book

A good way to prepare for your trial is to use a looseleaf binder or notebook to make a trial book that you will take with you to court. It will serve as a guidebook at your trial.

The first thing to go in your trial book should be a copy of your Notice of Claim. Read it again carefully to remind yourself exactly what you are claiming.

On the second page, draw a line down the centre of the page and write the word "Facts" at the top of the first column and "Evidence" at the top of the second. In the first column list each fact you will have to prove to make your case, and in the second column, opposite each fact, write down what evidence you will use to prove each one. That evidence may be your own testimony, it may be the testimony of another witness, or it may be a document such as a contract or a repair estimate.

If you are using papers or documents as evidence, try to have the originals if possible. Organize your papers in the order you will want to use them at trial and be sure you know what they say. You could keep them together in an envelope or clip each to a page in your book.

Make a page (or more if you need it) for the testimony of each witness. Your evidence will probably be the most important and it will be worth taking some time to prepare what you will say. You don't need to write down your testimony word for word, but make a list of the points you want to make.

Arrange the facts in logical order; usually the order in which they happened is the best way of telling the story. Be sure that you cover each fact you must prove, but also be sure to stick to the case. The judge will be very interested to hear what you have to say, but only if it directly relates to the case. The judge will not want to hear a lot of background about previous dealings you may have had with your opponent or about what kind of person he or she is.

Decide what witnesses besides yourself you will need, if any. The procedure for making sure they attend the trial is described in section **e.** below. If possible, you should speak to your witnesses before the trial date and let them know what the case is about, if they don't know, and what questions you intend to ask them. There is nothing wrong with this, or even with practising your questions and answers together, as long as you don't ask the witness for anything other than the truth. You should make sure your witness knows that this practice is quite proper and there is no reason to deny that he or she discussed the case with you, if the question comes up at the trial.

You may also want to think about some questions you will want to ask the defendant when he or she gives evidence. If you have a pretty good idea of what the defendant is likely to say, you can list some questions to ask. Otherwise, just leave a blank page where you could make some notes while the defendant is testifying.

If the defendant has made a counterclaim against you, look at the details and decide what, if anything, you agree with. For the rest, do you disagree with the claim itself, or only with the amount? For more discussion of how to respond to a counterclaim, see chapter 4.

You should also put into your trial book a copy of any other documents that have been filed in the case including the defendant's Reply, any certificates of service, and any Orders that may have been made.

By using a looseleaf notebook this way, you can put everything that has to do with your case together in an organized fashion. It will help you to prepare for your trial and you will feel more confident going to court when you know that you have everything you need at your fingertips.

d. IF YOU ARE THE DEFENDANT

A defendant can use a trial book in much the same way as described above. You will make a plan, organize your evidence, and make your notes.

Look carefully at the Notice of Claim and think about what your defence will be to each claim. You can assume that the claimant will probably begin by telling his or her side of the story, so give particular attention to the questions you will ask when it is your turn to cross-examine him or her.

e. WITNESSES

Often the people who you want to bring to court to give evidence for you will be quite willing to help you out. They may be family members, or employees, or neighbors. In that case, all you need to do is let them know when and where the trial is.

Other people may not show up unless required to do so. For these people you will need a summons. (There may be others who are glad to testify for you but still need a summons because, for example, their employer may require it in order to let them off work.)

You can get a Summons to Witness form from any Small Claims Court registry (see Sample #15). Fill it out and serve it on the witness at least seven days before the date the person is to testify, along with reasonable travel expenses.

You are permitted to serve the summons by ordinary mail, but you will have to allow fourteen days from the date of mailing, plus the seven-day notice period. If you want to be sure the person gets the summons, you should use personal service or registered mail. That way, if the witness does not appear, you will be able to prove to the judge that the summons was properly served. If you do that, and if the judge decides that the witness is necessary, the judge can order that the witness be arrested and brought to court.

It is hard to say exactly what is meant by "reasonable travelling expenses" because they will vary from one situation to another. If the trial is in the same community where the witness lives or works, bus fare will probably be what is required. The important thing to remember is that this amount must be offered to the witness at the same time the summons is served.

f. SETTLING THE CASE

No matter how much work you have done preparing for a trial, remember that the object of the exercise is to resolve the dispute, and it's never too late to do that. You may make or accept an offer to settle the case at any time, even after the trial has started.

If you do settle the case before trial but after a date has been set, just remember to notify the court registry that you won't need the trial date.

g. SUMMARY

If necessary, you can apply to change the trial date; you may also make changes in your documents in preparation for trial. The best way to prepare for trial is to organize your thoughts

SAMPLE #15
SUMMONS TO WITNESS

SUMMONS TO WITNESS
IN THE PROVINCIAL COURT OF BRITISH COLUMBIA (SMALL CLAIMS COURT)

FORM 8 (RULE 9)
SCL 008 (11 90)

REGISTRY FILE NUMBER
13141516
REGISTRY LOCATION
Vancouver

TO:
Fill in the name and address of the person you are requiring to come to court.

NAME Peter Spencer
ADDRESS 52 Howard Street
CITY TOWN MUNICIPALITY Vancouver   PROV B.C.   POSTAL CODE V2M 3L7   TEL. 686-2431

FROM:
Fill in the name of the party who requires the witness to attend.

You have been summoned as a witness by
Ruth Ryder

Copy the names of all parties in the case as shown on the Notice of Claim.

In the case between:

DENNIS DRIVER   DEFENDANT(S)

and

RUTH RYDER   CLAIMANT(S)

Fill in the date and place of the hearing.

You are required to attend the Provincial Court of British Columbia

on June _month_ 19 _day_ 199- _year_ at 10 A M _time_   or as soon after this time as the court schedule allows.

at 814 Richards Street, Vanvouver _court location_

If you want the witness to bring to court any records or other things list them here.

You are required to bring the following records and other things:

What must you do if you are served with a summons?
You must
   a) attend court at the time and place stated on the summons, and
   b) bring to court any records and other things required by the summons.

Can the summons be cancelled?
If you are not needed as a witness or it would be a hardship for you to attend court, a judge may cancel the summons.

What happens if you do not attend?
A judge may issue a warrant for your arrest.

You must provide the witness with reasonable travelling expenses.

The amount of $3.00   is attached for use as travelling expenses to enable you to come to the Court.

Sign and date your summons.

March _month_   15 _day_   199- _year_   _Ruth Ryder_ _signature of person issuing summons_

originator copy

and evidence by making a trial book. After analyzing your case to decide what facts you must prove, you will decide what evidence you will use to prove each fact. If you need documents, you will organize them in your book. If you need witnesses, you will consider whether they should be summoned, and you will prepare them for the trial. At the same time as you are working toward your trial date, you should also look for any opportunity to settle the case without going to court.

10
THE TRIAL

a. IF THE CLAIMANT DOES NOT ATTEND

If the claimant doesn't show up at the trial, the judge can dismiss the claim. That will end the case, except that the defendant can ask the judge to award costs against the claimant. This will usually amount to whatever witness fees and travel costs are applicable.

If you are the claimant and you know you are not going to be able to make it to the trial, try to get the other side to agree to another date. At the very least, notify the court registry, by letter if there is time and by telephone if there is not, that you can't be there. (See chapter 9 on changing the date.)

If you don't notify anyone — perhaps you made a mistake about the date and realize later that you have missed the trial date — it still might not be too late. You need to immediately apply to cancel the judge's order dismissing your claim. The procedure is the same as for cancelling a default order (see chapter 5).

If there is a counterclaim against a claimant who does not appear, the result is the same as where the defendant does not attend the trial (see **b.** below). In this case, the claimant is actually a defendant in the case of the counterclaim.

b. IF THE DEFENDANT DOES NOT ATTEND

If the defendant does not attend the trial, the claimant can ask the judge to make a Default Order. If the claim is for a specified amount, the Order will likely be made in that amount. If the claim is for damages, the claimant will have to prove the amount. Costs can also be awarded against the defendant. (See chapter 5 for more information on Default Orders and how they can be cancelled.)

If a defendant who does not appear has filed a counter-claim, the claimant can ask the judge to dismiss the counter-claim.

c. THE COURTROOM

Courtrooms are public places and except in very unusual circumstances, you are free to come and go from the room.

You may notice that lawyers give a slight bow or nod of the head toward the judge when entering or leaving the courtroom. This is expected from lawyers, but for anyone else, simple courtesy and respect is all that is asked. For example, although you may enter and leave the room while court is in session, you should try to make your entrances and exits during breaks in the proceedings (e.g., between cases or between witnesses).

The judge will sit at the front of the courtroom facing everyone else. In front of the judge is a table or desk where the court clerk keeps track of the flow of cases and paperwork.

To one side is the witness stand where you and the other witnesses will sit or stand to give evidence. Usually the judge will invite a witness to sit down, but you should stand until then. If this is a hardship for you, by all means ask if you may sit.

There will be another table (sometimes two) and chairs where the parties and their lawyers (if there are any) may sit, facing the judge. You are expected to stand any time you speak in court and any time the judge is speaking to you. It is considered disrespectful to remain seated while the judge speaks to you. (Again, if it is difficult for you to stand or to get up and down, just explain this to the judge.) The rest of the courtroom is taken up with seats for the public.

You may be wondering what you should wear to court. Whatever you would normally wear to work or to a business appointment will probably be appropriate. Don't feel you have to "dress up" for court, but as a matter of respect you should be sure your clothes are clean and tidy.

d. PROCEDURE

Each court in each location has its own features, but procedures are generally the same from one Small Claims Court to another.

1. Trial day

Try to arrive in plenty of time. You will feel more relaxed and confident. It's true that the cases are all set to start at the same time and so some people will have to wait, but you might be lucky enough to get your case on early. If you do have to wait, you can use the time to advantage by watching how others present their cases.

When the judge enters the courtroom, everyone stands. Then, the first thing that usually happens is that the list of cases is read. The parties stand up to identify themselves as their names are called. They will be asked to say whether they are ready to go ahead with the trial.

Then the trials will begin. Some judges try to hear the shortest cases first. Others will take the cases in the order they appear on the list.

2. The trial

A Small Claims Court trial does not always follow the formal pattern of most trials. A judge has the choice of running the trial according to the formal rules of evidence and procedure or not. When lawyers are involved for both sides, the formal rules will be followed. But when non-lawyers are acting for themselves, the judge will relax the formal rules to the extent necessary for fairness and efficiency. For example, judges often eliminate cross-examination. The judge asks each party to explain his or her case and then gives the party a chance to reply to anything

said. Usually a judge will announce this procedure at the beginning of the trial, but if he or she does not, you may ask for it.

Following is an explanation of the basic trial procedure,
and if you are familiar with it, you will be prepared for
whatever happens.

(a) Introduce yourself

When the name of your case is called for trial, walk to the front
of the courtroom and introduce yourself to the judge: "I am
Anne Miller and I am the claimant," for example. The other
party (in this case, the defendant), will do the same.

Your witnesses stay in their seats until they are called to
give their evidence or asked to leave the courtroom.

(b) Preliminary applications

Sometimes you will have to make what is called a "preliminary application" before the trial can begin. Usually these
matters will have been dealt with at the settlement conference,
but it may be that someone will have to apply to amend
(change) a Notice of Claim or a Reply, for example. If the
change is a major one, the judge may refuse to allow it. Or,
the judge may allow the change but adjourn the trial so that
the other side can prepare to meet the new claim or defence.
(In that case you will likely be required to pay the other side's
extra expenses for having to return on another day.) Or, the
change may be allowed and the case allowed to proceed. If
you know you are going to be asking for an amendment to
your claim or defence, you will be in a better position if you
have notified the other side in advance.

If you have such an application to make, you may simply
say to the judge, after the introductions are made, "Before we
begin, I would like the court's permission to apply for a
change to the Notice of Claim (for example). Then you will
tell the judge exactly what it is you want and why. If you can
assure the judge that the other side knew about your application in advance, you will be more likely to get your order.

(c) Opening statement

Once any preliminary applications are dealt with, the judge may ask the claimant to begin the case. If the judge asks for an opening statement, the claimant should tell the judge briefly what the case is about. For example, in a contract case, the claimant might say —

> Your Honour, this case is about a contract between the defendant and me. I agreed to do certain work and the defendant agreed to pay me. I did the work but I haven't been paid.

(d) Agreed facts

In most cases there are certain facts that can be agreed on in advance. These probably will have been discussed at the settlement conference. Either side can write down a list of facts and ask the other party to agree to them. These could then be read to the judge during the opening. For example, both sides might agree about the fact that the contract was made between them and that they both signed it. Then the claimant could just hand the contract to the judge and say —

> The defendant agrees that this is the contract and that she signed it. What we disagree about is whether I did the work as agreed in the contract.

In the case of a car accident, the claimant and defendant can probably agree about who was driving which car, the registration numbers, and perhaps where the cars were and the directions they were travelling just before the accident. Those facts could all be listed on a piece of paper, signed by both parties, and then read or handed to the judge.

The claimant should also tell the judge, during the opening statement, about any issues that were settled at the settlement conference.

(e) Excluding witnesses

If either side has witnesses present who could give different versions of the facts, either party should ask the judge to order that all witnesses remain outside the courtroom until they are called to testify. This is to prevent witnesses listening to each other and then shaping their own testimony accordingly. This order will be made automatically, but someone must remember to ask for it. Just say —

> Your Honour, I ask for an order excluding witnesses.

You might explain this to your witnesses beforehand, so they won't be surprised or offended when asked to leave the courtroom.

(f) The claimant's case

Now it is time for the claimant to call the first witness. In most cases, this is the claimant him or herself. Each witness is first sworn to tell the truth. If, for religious reasons, you do not wish to swear on the Bible, simply tell the judge and you will be asked to "affirm" instead.

If you are the claimant and you are beginning with your evidence, this is your chance to tell your story. Remember that the judge knows nothing about you or the other people involved. Stick to the facts of the case but don't leave out information that the judge will need in order to understand your claim. It's usually best to start at the beginning and tell what happened. If you prepared a summary of your evidence for your trial book, you will have already organized your thoughts and will be well prepared to give your evidence. You cannot read your notes, but if you have a record of certain dates or numbers or other items that you won't be able to recall from memory, you can ask the judge if you may refer to your book if the need arises.

After the claimant is finished, it is the defendant's turn to question (cross-examine) the claimant. (Cross-examination is discussed later in this chapter.)

If new issues come up in cross-examination, the claimant may respond to those after the defendant's questions are finished. But this is not the time for the claimant to bring up new evidence.

If the claimant has other witnesses, they will then be called to give their testimony. Just tell the judge the name of the witness you want next and the clerk will see that the person is brought in, if they are outside the courtroom. If you have more than one witness, think about calling them in logical order.

When a witness has taken the stand, it is up to the claimant to question (examine) the witness. Again, if you have made a summary in your trial book of the points you want to cover with the witness, and have gone over it together, you will both be well prepared. Have the trial book in front of you and check off the points as you cover them, so you won't miss anything essential. But be sure to listen for the answers instead of just reading a list of questions.

Again, the defendant then has the opportunity to cross-examine the witness. If new matters come up, you may ask to re-examine on those points after the cross-examination is finished.

(g) The defendant's case

When the claimant's witnesses are done it is the defendant's turn to present the other side. The defendant may give an opening statement, briefly telling the judge what is disputed and why.

Then the defendant's witnesses are called, usually beginning with the defendant, and are examined by the defendant and cross-examined by the claimant.

(h) Arguments

When all the evidence has been presented, the judge will ask the claimant for oral argument, or for summing up. Then it will be the defendant's turn. In argument, each side tries to summarize the case to its own best advantage, pointing up the strengths of its own case and the weaknesses in the other. The argument must be based on the evidence as it was given in court and cannot include any new evidence.

Normally the judge will announce his or her decision after both sides have finished their arguments. If the judge needs to take time to consider the case, you will be notified of the date the decision is to be given. However, you need not attend court again on that date unless you want to.

e. RULES OF EVIDENCE

There are many rules of evidence. Some are found in the provincial Evidence Act; others have developed as judges make rulings in individual cases. Even lawyers with long experience in the courtroom still struggle with some of the rules of evidence and no lay person should expect to master them.

In Small Claims Court, most judges do not insist that all rules of evidence be strictly followed. However, there are some that are very important and that you may hear being referred to in the course of the trial, especially if there is a lawyer involved.

The following discussion will give you a general idea of some of the rules that are most commonly encountered.

1. Hearsay

The rule against hearsay evidence is designed to prevent the use of second- and third-hand evidence. For example, if the issue was whether a car went through a red light, a witness would not be allowed to tell the court "My wife said she saw the car go through the red light." Instead, the wife would have to give that evidence herself.

The rule makes sense because we all know that as stories are repeated they often change or become distorted. Also, the person making the statement is not there to be cross-examined. The wife might be asked, for example: How close were you to the scene? From what angle could you see the light? Was the sun shining in your eyes? It might be that her statement could be quite successfully challenged if she were called on to defend it.

Hearsay also refers to *written* statements by another. For example, witnesses cannot testify about something they read in a book or in the newspaper.

Sometimes witnesses *are* allowed to report what someone else told them if the evidence is not given for the purpose of proving that the statement was true.

For example, suppose you were involved in an intersection accident with a driver who you say was driving much too fast. When he got out of his car the other driver exclaimed: "I was already a half hour late for my appointment!" A witness who heard him say that would be allowed to tell that in court. It would not be hearsay because the point is not to prove that the man was late for his appointment. Rather, the point is to prove that he thought he was late and was therefore probably hurrying and driving too fast.

This is an example of evidence that sounds like hearsay but is not. There are many other kinds of evidence that are, in fact, hearsay, but are allowable under one of the many exceptions to the hearsay rule. These exceptions are very complicated. Your best bet in dealing with hearsay evidence is this: if you hear a witness telling the court about something someone else has said or written, stand up immediately and say to the judge "Your Honour, I object to this evidence because it is hearsay." The judge will decide whether it is admissible or not.

On the other hand, you may have some evidence you want to use but are unsure about whether it's hearsay or not. If it is important to your case, you might consider getting some legal advice. However, a few of the more common exceptions are discussed briefly here, to guide you.

(a) Repair estimates and appraisals

The major exception to the hearsay rule in Small Claims Court applies to written repair estimates and valuations or appraisals. If you are going to use a written estimate or appraisal, just be sure it is from an established professional and that it is signed by someone in authority.

(b) Statements against interest

A witness can testify about a statement made by one of the parties to the case *if the statement goes against the interests of the person who made it.*

Suppose that after a car accident a witness hears the driver of one of the cars say "I just looked away for a moment and I didn't see the light was red till it was too late." The witness would be allowed to give that evidence.

However, if the driver had said "It wasn't my fault, I was obeying the speed limit and driving carefully," then evidence of that statement would not be allowed.

The reason is that normally people will not say something that goes against their own interests unless it is true. But people may say things in their own favor for many reasons.

Be careful with this one, though. If you want to introduce evidence of a statement made against your interest by another party, you must introduce the whole of the statement and some of it may well benefit the other side or harm your case.

One other caution: if the statement was made in the course of trying to agree on a settlement, the statement won't be admissible at all. This is because the law tries to encourage people to compromise and to settle disputes without going to court unless necessary. People would not be willing to negotiate if everything they said during these discussions could be used against them in court. Lawyers often use the words "without prejudice" at the top of a letter written in the course of settlement discussions to emphasize that this letter cannot be used in evidence.

(c) Public or official documents

Statements made in public or official documents are admissible as proof of the facts recorded in them if the statements are made by an authorized person in the course of his or her duties or if the facts are of public interest or notoriety or are required to be recorded for the public benefit.

The most common examples are statutes, government gazettes, public records, surveys, assessments, official certificates, corporate records, company books, bankers' books, and works of reference.

(d) Evidence Act exceptions to the rule against hearsay

Other exceptions to the rule against hearsay are found in the Canada Evidence Act and the B.C. Evidence Act. These include medical reports and books and records kept in the ordinary course of business by companies that routinely keep such records. Hospital records for a patient are one example.

2. Direct examination

After a witness has been sworn in, it is the responsibility of the party whose witness it is to ask questions that will draw out the evidence that the witness has to give. This is called direct examination or examination in chief.

When you are examining your own witness, your aim is to ask the questions that will give the witness the chance to tell all the facts the witness knows about that will help to prove your case. If your witness is called because he or she is an expert in some subject (e.g., a doctor giving a medical opinion), you may be asking your witness for opinions as well as facts. This is discussed below in section **4**.

Generally speaking, you may not ask your own witness questions in a way that suggests the answer you want. These are called "leading questions".

For example, you may not ask "Wasn't the light red when the blue car entered the intersection?" Instead, you should say "What color was the light when the blue car entered the intersection?"

This rule is usually relaxed in the interests of efficiency when the witness is testifying about matters that are undisputed. For example, you would be allowed to say "Your name is Daphne Spencer and you live at 123 Main Street and you are 38 years old. Is that correct?"

But, when you get into matters that are in dispute, be careful about asking questions that are too long. You will do best if you break up your questions into single items so that each answer can be clearly understood.

While the other party's witnesses are giving their evidence "in chief," listen for inconsistencies, mistakes, or omissions that you can ask about in cross-examination. Make notes and use them when it is your turn to cross-examine.

3. Cross-examination

In cross-examination, the rules are quite different. Here you are questioning a witness who is not "on your side." You have two purposes:

   (a) to weaken, qualify, or destroy your opponent's case either by challenging the credibility (believability) of the witness, or by getting the witness to contradict or to qualify his or her earlier testimony; and

(b) to prove your own case by means of your opponent's witnesses.

Witnesses' credibility depends on several things: their knowledge of the facts; their interest in the result — that is, what they stand to gain or lose from the case; and their general reputation for honesty. You can test the credibility of a witness by asking:

(a) How does the witness know what he or she claims to know?

(b) What opportunity did the witness have to make the observations he or she says were made? (Where were they in relation to what happened and what were the conditions?)

(c) Does the witness have anything to gain or lose from the case? (For example, is the witness employed by the party?)

Think about the questions you will ask and think about what evidence you could use to contradict any untruthful answers you might get.

It can also be important to go over the witness' evidence that was given in direct examination to point out any errors or inconsistencies or improbabilities. If you listened carefully to the direct examination and made notes, be sure to look them over and check that you have covered everything before you end your questioning and sit down.

You do not have to limit your questions in cross-examination to issues that were discussed in the witness' direct examination. You can ask about any facts that are relevant to the case. You also can ask about anything that might not be strictly related to the case but would call into question the credibility of the witness. For example, if the witness has a criminal record, you can ask about that. If the witness has told a different version of the story on another occasion, you can ask about that.

You also may ask leading questions on cross-examination. For example, you could say, "It was raining very hard at the time of the accident, wasn't it?" (If you were asking your own witness, you would have to say: "And what was the weather like at the time of the accident?")

You may not, however, try to mislead the witness with leading questions. For example, the question about the rain would not be proper if you knew that the accident happened on a sunny day.

If you choose not to cross-examine a witness, the judge will usually assume that you accept the witness' evidence. Sometimes this is the best choice to make. If the evidence has not really hurt your case and you know that you are not likely to get the witness to change his or her evidence, you are often better off to leave it alone rather than give the witness the chance to reinforce it.

If you are calling witnesses, you should warn them about cross-examination and caution them not to become angry or to get into arguments with the person asking the questions. The following is the advice you should give your witnesses about cross-examination (and the advice you should heed yourself when you are being examined):

(a) Stay calm and take your time in answering.

(b) Face the judge and address your answers to the judge, no matter who is asking the questions.

(c) If you don't understand a question, say so and ask to have it repeated or rephrased.

(d) Be respectful and don't argue with or criticize or insult the questioner.

(e) If you don't know the answer to a question, say so.

4. Expert evidence

Most witnesses are called to give evidence about facts that they know. Some, however, are called to give opinions about matters in which they have expertise. A common example would be a doctor who is called to give an opinion about what might have caused a particular injury, or what the chances are of complete recovery. Another expert might be called to say at what speed a car was likely travelling when an accident occurred.

There are special rules about expert evidence. If you plan to call an expert to give opinion evidence, you must give the other parties a written summary of the evidence at least 14 days in advance. This gives the other side time to prepare to cross-examine your expert or to find its own expert.

If you are unable to get the expert's summary to the other side 14 days ahead of time, and you don't want to ask for an adjournment of the trial, deliver it to the other parties as soon as you can. The judge can allow expert opinion evidence to be given even without 14 days notice and may do so if the other side has not been unfairly disadvantaged.

Many times you can simply use the expert's written report itself without calling the witness to testify. This is often done, for example, with doctors' reports. But you must serve a copy of the report (not just a summary of the evidence) to the other side at least 14 days in advance. Again, exceptions can be made, but it's best to try to stay within the time limits.

If you receive an expert report from your opponent you may decide that you would like to question the writer of the report. If so, then at least seven days before the trial you may notify the other party, in writing, that you require the expert to attend the trial for cross-examination.

Be careful with this, though. If the judge decides that you insisted on bringing the expert to court unnecessarily, you may have to pay the expert's expenses.

An exception to the requirement of advance notice is made for repair estimates and estimates of value (appraisals). These can be introduced as evidence even though they were not served on the other party.

5. Documents

If you have documents that you want to use as evidence, see if the other party will agree that they can be admitted as evidence without having to formally prove each one. This can save time and expense. You could ask about this at the settlement conference.

If the documents are not agreed to, they must be properly proven, unless they come within the "official documents" exception to the rule against hearsay. An example of such an exception is a certificate of judgment from a court in another province or a marriage licence.

Otherwise, you will have to prove that the document really is what it purports to be. How you do this depends on the circumstances. If you want to enter a photograph, you normally have to call as a witness the person who took the picture. (However, note that in ICBC cases, photos of the damaged vehicles can be obtained from ICBC and the adjuster need not attend.) Other types of documents may be proven through the testimony of someone who signed it.

To prove the admissibility of a contract, you could call as a witness one of the parties to the contract and say:

> Q: I am showing you a contract signed by two people, one of whom appears to be Diane Owen. Is that your signature, Mrs. Owen?
> A: Yes.

> Q: And is this the written version of the contract you made with Robert Laurie on June 9, 199-?
> A: Yes.

Q: And whose is the other signature on the contract?

A: Mr. Laurie's. I saw him sign it.

In most cases you must produce the original of a document and not a copy. However, there are exceptions to this too. For example, a certified copy of the registration of a vehicle, provided by the Motor Vehicles branch to prove ownership of a vehicle would be admissible.

f. A TYPICAL TRIAL

This section looks at a typical Small Claims case and describes how the trial would proceed. Many Small Claims cases result from car accidents. ICBC insures both parties, so the issue usually is the deductible which one party feels should be paid by the other.

In our example, there was an accident in an intersection. Both drivers insist that the other went through a red light.

There are generally five things the claimant must prove:

(a) **The authority (jurisdiction) of the court to hear this claim.** (It must have some connection to British Columbia.) Do this by evidence of where the accident took place, or where the defendant lives.

(b) **The identity of the owners of the vehicles involved.** (Normally the drivers will have exchanged registration information at the scene.)

(c) **The identity of the drivers of the vehicles.** You can do this by pointing out the person in the courtroom. (If the driver of the car was not also the owner, both should be named as defendants in the action.)

(d) **Liability of the defendant;** that is, that the negligence of the owner or driver of the car was the cause of the accident. (This is usually proven through the testimony of the claimant and witnesses and the cross-examination of the defendant and his or her witnesses.)

(e) **The amount of the damages incurred.** (This is usually done by submitting two or three written and signed repair estimates from reputable garages. Even though these are strictly speaking, hearsay evidence, they are generally accepted in Small Claims Court.)

During the course of the trial, the claimant will probably lead evidence (both his or her own and that of witnesses) to prove these facts:

(a) Date and time of the accident

(b) Direction each car was travelling

(c) The point at which the claimant first saw the defendant

(d) What happened from that time to the time of the accident

(e) Location of the accident with full description of the intersection including number of lanes of traffic in each direction, position of parked cars, position of the traffic lights, and other details. (A diagram might help with this.)

(f) Weather conditions, visibility, time of sunset or sunrise if relevant

(g) Density and speed of other traffic

(h) Any steps the claimant took to avoid impact, such as braking or swerving, or any conditions such as oncoming traffic that might have prevented such action

(i) Location of each vehicle after the impact

(j) Location and extent of damage to the claimant's car

(k) Location and extent of damage to the defendant's car if that is in dispute

(l) Any conversation that the claimant and the defendant driver may have had immediately following the accident

(m) The names of any witnesses to the accident.

If a police officer attended at the scene of the accident, his or her testimony can be helpful. You should begin by calling the police department involved and ask what the fee is for a police report. If they cannot take your request over the telephone, write a letter (see Sample #16).

When you receive the report, look it over carefully and see if it contains information that would be helpful to your case. If so, you will have to summons the police officer to testify at the trial. (You can't use the report itself because it is hearsay.)

If you see that the defendant was charged as a result of the accident, check with the court to find out what the result was. If there was a conviction, you will want to ask the defendant about this when you are cross-examining.

Automobile accident cases, like many others, often are decided on the basis of the judge's opinion about the credibility of the two parties and their witnesses. The secret is to prepare yourself and your witnesses to give clear, logical, and truthful testimony.

In our car accident example, if neither side presents a particularly strong case, the judge may very well divide liability between the two. Often the result is a 50/50 split. If the claimant has sued for payment of a $500 deductible and the defendant has counterclaimed for $250, this would mean the claimant pays the defendant $125 and the defendant pays the claimant $250. Each would be responsible for his or her own expenses.

g. SUMMARY

Once the trial begins, it is useful to know what to expect. If you remain respectful, you should have no problem and the judge will help you through the trial. You will begin with your opening statement, and then you will question your witnesses and cross-examine the other party's witnesses. When questioning, it is important not to use hearsay evidence as that will be disallowed. There are special rules about expert evidence and proving documents.

City of Vancouver Police Department
312 Main Street
Vancouver, B.C.
V6A 2T2

Attention: Traffic Records Dept.

Re: Automobile Accident Report

I was involved in an accident with another automobile on September 8, 199-, at the intersection of Main Street and 33rd Avenue at about 10 a.m. My name is Tim Park and the licence number of my car is B.C. HFD 2J2. The driver of the other car is Chris Richardson and her licence number is B.C. XF4 256. The investigating officer was P.C. McKay, and her badge number is 5446.

I would appreciate receiving a copy of P.C. McKay's report. I enclose a cheque for your fee.

Yours truly,

Tim Park

Tim Park

11
THE RESULT

a. THE JUDGMENT

1. The payment order

The judge usually gives his or her decision (judgment) immediately following the end of the trial. In any case where the
decision is that one side must pay the other, the judge is
required to lead a discussion, right then at the end of the trial,
about payment of the debt. (Once there is a court order
requiring one person to pay money to another, the person
who must pay is called the "debtor" and the one who is to
receive the money is called the "creditor.")

The judge will ask the debtor if he or she needs time to
pay. The object is to arrive at a reasonable schedule for payment — one that the debtor can meet and that is fair to the
creditor. The debtor might propose a series of instalment
payments, or it may simply be a delayed payment date. Then
the judge will ask whether the creditor agrees with the proposal. If so, the judge will make that schedule part of the order.

If the creditor does not agree, the judge will likely ask
some questions to determine whether each side is being reasonable. Then the judge has three choices. He or she may:

(a) Order a payment hearing for a later date (see section
c. below)

(b) Order a payment schedule (This may or may not be
the one proposed by the debtor earlier in the discussion.)

(c) Order no payment schedule (In that case the entire amount is due immediately.)

If a claim is being made against you, you should come to court prepared to discuss your financial situation and propose a payment schedule. Do this even if you do not expect to lose your case.

2. Reserved judgment

Occasionally, the judge wants to take some time to think about the case, or maybe to do some research on the legal issues involved. The judge will then "reserve" judgment. If judgment is given at a later date and the parties are not present, the entire amount is due immediately. (But see section c. below on requesting a payment hearing at which time a payment schedule may be proposed.)

3. Limitations of the judgment

Keep in mind that the court is not a collection agency. If you win your case and get an order saying money is to be paid to you, in many cases the debtor will simply pay. But if not, it will be up to you to take whatever steps are necessary to collect that money. (See chapter 13.)

On the other hand, the Small Claims Court — much more than the other courts — does get involved in the enforcement of its own orders. The court doesn't collect your money for you, but it gives you the tools you need to do the job.

The Small Claims Court procedures promote a resolution that increases the likelihood that judgments will be paid. The key features of this approach are the payment schedule and the payment hearing.

b. THE PAYMENT SCHEDULE

The payment schedule recognizes that if a person is ordered to pay an amount that is simply impossible, that person is likely to resist paying at all. Many "successful" parties have spent far more than the case was ever worth in trying to collect judgments from people who couldn't pay. However, if the order is put in terms (e.g., an instalment schedule), that is more or less realistic from the debtor's point of view, the chances are much greater that the amount will eventually be paid.

A payment schedule can be very important to both parties. For the debtor, it means that as long as the terms of the schedule are obeyed — all payments are made on time — the creditor cannot take any steps, such as garnishment or seizing goods, to collect the debt. For the creditor, it means a much better chance of actually receiving what is owed.

c. THE PAYMENT HEARING

1. When a payment hearing may be requested

As stated above, the judge may order a payment hearing at the time of judgment. This may be because a payment schedule cannot be ordered immediately after the decision because the parties don't have the necessary information at the time.

Payment hearings can also be requested by either party in the case. If you are the debtor (you've been ordered to pay money to someone) you might want to ask for one, for example, if there is already a payment schedule in effect but your situation has changed and you find you can no longer make the payments (even if there has already been a previous payment hearing). Or maybe the judge's decision was given some time after the trial (reserved) and you weren't present to ask for a payment schedule at the time.

If you are the creditor, you may want your debtor to come to a payment hearing and provide information about his or her financial situation so that you can take other enforcement action. For example, you might learn that the debtor has assets you didn't know about. You could ask for a payment hearing at which you might ask that the debt be paid at once or in larger installments. Or maybe no payment schedule was set when judgment was given because the parties weren't present so you want to request a payment hearing to set one.

(A payment hearing may also be used long before a case goes to trial. If the defendant files a Reply admitting the debt but asking for time to pay, the case can go directly to a payment hearing.)

2. What happens at the payment hearing?

A payment hearing is basically an inquiry into the financial circumstances of the debtor. It is less formal than a trial.

If the debtor is not there, a warrant for his or her arrest is ordered if there was personal service and an affidavit has been sworn. If the creditor is not there, and it is his or her application, the payment hearing is cancelled.

If both parties are present, usually the judge will ask the debtor if he or she has a payment proposal. If so, the creditor may accept it or propose something else.

If the parties don't agree, then the creditor will begin by asking questions (see below). If the hearing has been requested by the debtor, he or she will begin by explaining the reason for the hearing and then describe his or her situation. In either case, the creditor will be allowed to question the debtor. The judge may ask questions too.

The debtor can be asked about his or her employment and other income; bank accounts, property and other assets; debts owed *to* the debtor and debts owed *by* the debtor. The debtor can also be asked about any assets that he or she has sold or disposed of in any way since the claim arose (not just since the trial).

The debtor should come prepared with pay slips, copies of income tax statements, bank statements, and any other documents that will support the debtor's own evidence.

The creditor should come prepared with a list of questions to ask. They will usually be along these lines:

(a) Where do you work? (Get the employer's name and address)

(b) How much do you earn?

(c) What day are you paid?

(d) Do you have income from any other source?

(e) What bank accounts do you have? (Ask for name of bank, branch, account numbers and balances.)

(f) Do you have a car? (Ask for make, model, year, and registration number.)

(g) Do you own your home?

(h) Do you have an interest in a business?

(i) Do you own any savings bonds or other investments?

(j) What other assets do you have?

(k) Does anyone owe you any money?

Obviously, if the answer to any of these is "Yes," you would follow up by asking for more detail. You may have information from other sources too that will lead you to ask other questions.

3. The outcome

After hearing what everyone has to say, the judge may make a payment schedule setting out the dates and amounts of payments to be made. If there already has been a payment schedule ordered, this may be changed.

Or, the judge can decide to make no order. In that case, the full amount of the judgment is due at once.

4. How a creditor asks for a payment hearing

If you are the creditor and you want a payment hearing, ask at the registry for the form Summons to a Payment Hearing (see Sample #17). Fill it out, file a copy at the registry and serve it on the debtor at least seven days before the date of the hearing. The registry will provide you with the date of the hearing to fill in on the form. (**Note:** The Summons must be served in person with a sworn affidavit of service filed. This procedure has recently changed and, at the time of writing, was not included in the Small Claims Rules. Contact the registry for more information.)

The summons must be directed to a person, not a company or partnership, because it is a person who must attend and answer questions. If the debtor is a company or partnership you should think about who it is you want to be able to question. If it is information about a company's assets you want, for example, think about who in the company would have that information. You can summon an officer, director, or employee of the company. If the debtor is a partnership, choose one of the partners.

You can add a requirement to the summons that the person bring to the hearing company records or other documents that will contain the information you need.

5. How the debtor asks for a payment hearing

If you are a debtor and want a payment hearing, ask the registry for a Notice of a Payment Hearing (see Sample #18), and fill it out and file a copy at the registry. The registry will provide you with the date of the hearing to fill in on the form. Then you must serve the Notice on the creditor at least seven days before the hearing date.

If you want a payment hearing because the judge has reserved judgment and you expect that a payment order may be made against you and you want time to pay, try to attend when the decision is given. Then you can immediately ask for a payment hearing and ask the judge to order that no enforcement steps be taken until after the hearing. If you cannot attend, then contact the registry and ask to have a payment hearing scheduled as soon as possible.

SAMPLE #17
SUMMONS TO PAYMENT HEARING

SUMMONS TO A PAYMENT HEARING

IN THE PROVINCIAL COURT OF BRITISH COLUMBIA (SMALL CLAIMS COURT)

REGISTRY FILE NUMBER
9101112
REGISTRY LOCATION
Richmond

FORM 12 (RULE 12)

TO:
Fill in the name, address and telephone number of the person you are requiring to come to court.

NAME Jay Bookkeeper
ADDRESS 98 34th Avenue

CITY, TOWN
MUNICIPALITY Richmond   B.C.   V6N 2H4   TEL '679-7660
PROV.   POSTAL CODE

Copy the names of all parties in the case as shown on the Payment or Default Order

You have been summoned to a payment hearing in the case between:

Jordan Homeowner   CREDITOR

and

Robertsons Roofers Ltd.   DEBTOR

Fill in the date, time and place of the hearing.

You are required to attend the Provincial Court of British Columbia

on September   9   199–   at   10   A   M   or as soon after this time as the court schedule allows.
    month   day   year   time

at   6931 Granville Avenue, Richmond
                    court location

You are required to bring the following records and other things:

List what you want the person to bring to court.

Income tax returns for Robertsons Roofers for 1990 and 1991

What happens at the payment hearing?
Evidence may be heard about any of the following:
a) the income and assets of the debtor;
b) the debts owed to and by the debtor;
c) any assets that the debtor has disposed of since the claim arose;
d) the means that the debtor has, or may have in the future, of paying the amount owed.

Can the summons be cancelled?
Any person who is served with a Summons to a Payment Hearing may apply to a judge who may
a) cancel the summons if the person is not the right person to provide information on behalf of the debtor, and
b) direct the registrar to issue a new summons to someone who is the right person to provide the information.

What happens if the person summoned does not attend?
If the creditor asks, the Judge can issue a warrant for the arrest of the person.

month   day   year   by the court

court copy

SUMMONS TO A PAYMENT HEARING

court copy

106

NOTICE OF A PAYMENT HEARING
IN THE PROVINCIAL COURT OF BRITISH COLUMBIA (SMALL CLAIMS COURT)

REGISTRY FILE NUMBER
45678
REGISTRY LOCATION
Prince George

FORM 13 (RULE 12)
SCL 043 (11/96)

TO:
Fill in the name, address and telephone number of the person you are notifying about the payment hearing.

NAME: Robin Gardiner
ADDRESS: 123 King Street
CITY, TOWN, MUNICIPALITY: Prince George PROV: B.C. POSTAL CODE: V6K 1L7 TEL: 269-1234

CREDITOR

FROM:
Fill in the name, address and telephone number of the debtor who is requesting the payment hearing.

NAME: Leslie Householder
ADDRESS: 789 Main Street
CITY, TOWN, MUNICIPALITY: Prince George PROV: B.C. POSTAL CODE: TEL: 378-5678

DEBTOR

A payment hearing will be held in the Provincial Court of British Columbia

on January 15 199– at 10 A.M. or as soon after this time as the court schedule allows.

at 1600 Third Avenue, Prince George
court location

What happens at the payment hearing?
Evidence may be heard about any of the following:
a) the income and assets of the debtor;
b) the debts owed to and by the debtor;
c) any assets that the debtor has disposed of since the claim arose;
d) the means that the debtor has, or may have in the future, of paying the amount owed.

The Judge may order a payment schedule specifying
a) the date by which the debt must be paid, or
b) the amounts and dates of installments.

If you do not not plan to attend, you should let the registry know that by letter.

What happens if a creditor does not attend the payment hearing?
The Judge may hold the hearing, cancel it or postpone it.

court copy

court copy

NOTICE OF A PAYMENT HEARING

SAMPLE #19
PAYMENT ORDER

PAYMENT ORDER

IN THE PROVINCIAL COURT OF BRITISH COLUMBIA (SMALL CLAIMS COURT)

FORM 10 (RULE 11)
SCL C10-11 90)

REGISTRY FILE NUMBER
45678
REGISTRY LOCATION
Prince George

In the case between

Fill in the name(s), address(es) and phone number(s) of the parties. Include a third party if one was named. Be careful to name the parties correctly.

NAME Robin Gardiner
ADDRESS 123 King Street

CITY, TOWN MUNICIPALITY Prince George   B.C. PROV.   V6K 1L7 POSTAL CODE   TEL 269-1234

CLAIMANT(S)

and

NAME Leslie Householder
ADDRESS 789 Main Street

CITY, TOWN MUNICIPALITY Prince George   B.C. PROV.   V6K 2M3 POSTAL CODE   TEL 378-5678

DEFENDANT(S)

and

NAME
ADDRESS

CITY, TOWN MUNICIPALITY   PROV.   POSTAL CODE   TEL #

THIRD PARTY

If the judge has ordered payment of money, fill in the name of the party ordered to pay (DEBTOR) and the name of the party the money is to be paid to (CREDITOR).

THIS COURT ORDERS Leslie Householder   **DEBTOR**

TO PAY TO Robin Gardiner   **CREDITOR** $ 240.00   Amount ordered by Judge

+ $ 35.00   Expenses allowed

+ $ 6.30   Interest

Check the appropriate box

☐ immediately, or

= $ 281.30   **TOTAL AMOUNT OF PAYMENT ORDER**

X☒ in accordance with the following payment schedule

If the judge has ordered payment by installments or before a fixed date, say what amounts are to be paid and when.

$100.00 to be paid on or before February 1, 199–
$100.00 to be paid on or before March 1, 199–
$ 81.30 to be paid on or before April 1, 199–

Has the judge ordered something other than the payment of money?

THIS COURT ORDERS

+ $ any expenses allowed

This will be signed and dated by the court.

month   day   year   by the court

For more information about enforcement proceedings there is a booklet called "Getting Results"

court copy

court copy

108

d. ENTERING THE ORDER

When a decision has been made on the trial, most court registries will prepare the formal order for the successful party, and will automatically "enter" it in the court records and send copies to the parties. Make sure you have a copy that has a stamp on it indicating that it has been entered (see Sample #19).

Check with your court registry to find out if you have to complete the Payment Order yourself or if they will do it for you.

e. SUMMARY

At the end of the trial, if the judge orders one party to pay money to another, the judge must ask right then if the debtor needs time to pay. If so, the judge will try to order a payment schedule that is fair to the creditor and that the debtor can handle. Whether or not a payment schedule is ordered at that time, either party may request a payment hearing for the purpose of setting a payment schedule or cancelling or changing one that's already been made.

12
APPEALS

a. WHO CAN APPEAL?

Any party in a small claims case can appeal a Small Claims Court judgment. (The rules covering appeals from Small Claims Court are found in the Small Claims Act.) However, this isn't a decision to be made lightly. The appeal will be to the Supreme Court of British Columbia, which means you will likely want to hire a lawyer. (Supreme Court procedures are quite different from Small Claims Court: the rules and forms are not designed for use by non-lawyers.)

It will cost money, with or without a lawyer, it will take time, and there is no guarantee that the result will be any better for you. In fact, it could be worse because you could end up being ordered to pay costs to the other side.

If you are considering appealing a Small Claims Court decision, you would do well to get some advice from a lawyer who will look at the evidence on both sides of the case and give you an opinion about your chances of success.

b. HOW TO APPEAL

To appeal a judgment, you must file a Notice of Appeal form, which you can get from any small claims registry. The appeal must be started within 40 days. The 40-day period starts the day after the date the Small Claims Court order was made.

Fill out the form and then file it in the Supreme Court registry nearest to the court where the order was made. If you are unsure which registry to use, ask at the Small Claims Court.

On the *same day* you must file a copy of that notice in the small claims registry as well.

c. DEPOSIT

When you appeal an order, you have to pay a $200 deposit. This will be held in court as security in case you lose the appeal and are ordered to pay costs to the other side.

Also, if you are appealing against an order that requires you to pay money to the other party, you will have to pay that full amount into court as well.

Suppose the claimant sues the defendant for $1 000 in damages and wins. If the defendant appeals, he or she must pay a $200 deposit as security against costs plus the $1 000, for a total of $1 200. If the defendant loses the appeal, the claimant will get the $1 000 plus whatever amount of the $200 he or she is entitled to for costs. If the costs awarded to the claimant are more than $200, then that amount will have to be collected separately, but at least the claimant will have the amount of the original judgment.

However, there is a provision to have the deposit reduced. If you cannot pay the amount or think that it would be unfair to require it, you can apply to the Supreme Court for a reduction.

d. SUSPENSION OF COLLECTION PROCEEDINGS

Once the required deposit and the Notice of Appeal have been filed, the Small Claims Court order, and any steps to enforce it, are suspended. That means that if you have won a judgment in Small Claims Court but the other side appeals, you may not go ahead and garnishee wages or do anything else until after the appeal is dealt with.

Normally this is not a real hardship. Although it will mean a delay, at least the money will be safely in the court and if you are successful at the appeal it will automatically be paid to you.

But there may be circumstances that make it unfair. Therefore, there is a provision for you to ask the court for permission to go ahead and try to enforce your judgment while the appeal proceeds. This application also is to the Supreme Court.

e. SETTING THE DATE FOR THE APPEAL

After you've filed your notice of appeal (or at the same time) you must ask the registry to set a date for the appeal to be heard. This date will be at least 21 days away.

f. SERVING THE NOTICE ON THE OTHER SIDE

Now it's time to let the other side know about your appeal. In fact, if you've been ordered to pay money, you'll want to do this as quickly as possible so the creditor will know to stop enforcement proceedings.

You must serve the notice on every party who is affected.

For example, say you were suing a contracting company and one of its employees. The judge dismissed both claims. You decide there is no point pursuing the case against the employee because the employee doesn't have any money anyway so you appeal the decision only with respect to the company. You must serve the notice on the company but not on the employee.

You have seven days to serve the Notice of Appeal after the date you filed it in the Supreme Court; and you have seven days to serve the Notice of Hearing after the date of your application to set a hearing date. In most cases it will simplify things if you apply for your hearing date at the time you file your Notice of Appeal. Then you can serve both documents together.

As soon as you've served both documents, you must file in the Supreme Court registry, an affidavit saying who served them, when and how they were served (whether personally or by registered mail) and on whom they were served.

g. THE APPEAL HEARING

The appeal will be an entirely new trial and it will be a more formal proceeding than in Small Claims court. You will most likely need a lawyer to represent you.

h. SUMMARY

There is a procedure for appealing a Small Claims Court judgment. The appeal is to the Supreme Court of British Columbia and it must be started within 40 days of the date the order was made. You would likely need the services of a lawyer for this procedure.

13
COLLECTING YOUR MONEY

If you have won your judgment and the debtor has not immediately paid, or made arrangements to pay, this is the time to take a hard look at your options. You will have to think seriously about how much money is involved and how much time, effort, and money you are willing to put into collecting it. Unless there are special circumstances, you will usually want to begin with the simplest and cheapest collection methods and work up from there. At some point, unfortunately, you may have to decide that it isn't worth pursuing the matter any further. That still doesn't mean you'll never get your money. It may just mean a longer wait.

The more information you have about the debtor's circumstances, the better chance you have of collecting your money.

(a) If the person has a job or bank account, you can try garnishment.

(b) If the person owns assets such as a car or truck or machinery, or even household goods, you can have them seized and sold.

(c) If the person owns an interest in real estate, you can register a Certificate of Judgment against it.

(d) If the debtor stubbornly refuses to pay, you can ultimately have the person sent to jail.

If you haven't already had a payment hearing, you should begin by taking that step because it is relatively simple and it won't cost anything except your time. Besides encouraging the debtor to pay, it will give you the information you need to pursue these other options if necessary. (See chapter 11 for a discussion on payment hearings.)

a. GARNISHMENT

If the court has ordered someone to pay you money, and he or she hasn't paid, garnishment is a collection method you should consider. Basically, it allows you to get hold of money that someone else owes to the debtor. This "someone else" could be the bank where the debtor has an account, or it could be the debtor's employer, or a client or customer of the debtor.

The rules governing garnishment are included in the Court Order Enforcement Act, but they can be quite difficult to understand. The Small Claims Court has forms for you to use and if you follow the instructions carefully you will be able to carry out a garnishment yourself.

1. What can be garnished?

Most often, creditors will garnish wages or a bank account. Bank accounts seem like easy targets and they can be. But a person who is really trying to avoid paying debts is unlikely to leave money lying around in a bank account.

If your debtor keeps a bank account under a trade or business name, you can try garnishing that account. It will be up to the bank manager to decide whether the debtor is actually the owner of the account. The same goes for joint accounts. You may or may not be successful, but if there is money in the account it is worth a try. You stand to lose only your time and some minor out-of-pocket expenses.

If the debtor has a job, it will be harder for him or her to hide wages from a creditor. However, the law exempts a certain portion of wages from garnishment. The purpose of the exemptions is to ensure that the person has enough left to live on and to support his or her dependants. Generally, 70%

of wages or salary, after the normal payroll deductions, is exempt from garnishment.

However, there are minimum amounts for the protection of low wage earners. In the case of a person without dependants, a minimum of $100 per month is protected from garnishment. In the case of a debtor with one or more dependants, the minimum is $200 per month. (If the pay period is shorter, these amounts are reduced pro rata: that is, about $25 or $50 per week.)

The Court Order Enforcement Act does allow these amounts to be varied under special circumstances. For a low wage earner, the $100 and $200 exemptions can only be varied upwards; that is, to the benefit of the debtor. In other cases, the percentage exemption can be varied in either direction. However, in no case will more than 90% of the debtor's wages be protected from garnishment.

There are exceptions here, if the debt was incurred for board or lodging. The law presumes that if that is the case, the person's basic living needs are already being taken care of. The $100 exemption for the single person does not apply and the $200 exemption will not apply if a judge is satisfied that the $200 is not necessary for the support and maintenance of the debtor's dependants.

A creditor or debtor who wants to raise or lower the exemption figures must apply to a judge, giving full reasons for the application.

The trouble with garnishing wages is that each garnishment is good for only one pay day. However, if the debtor realizes that you intend to do this every time, he or she may agree to ask the employer to automatically deduct a certain amount from each pay cheque and send it to you.

2. How to garnish

(a) Forms

Ask the Small Claims Court registry for a Garnishing Order After Judgment and an Affidavit in Support of Garnishing Order After Judgment (see Samples #20 and #21). The forms ask you to fill in the date and amount of the court order you are enforcing, the amount still owing, and the name and address of the garnishee. The garnishee is the one who owes money to the debtor: the debtor's bank or employer, for example.

Take both completed forms to the court registry where the registrar will insert the amount of costs you may be allowed to collect, sign the order, and give you back the copies you will need.

(b) Serving the forms

You then must serve the documents on the garnishee. You can pay a professional process server to do this for you or you can do it yourself. You can also use registered mail if you wish, but be sure to ask the post office for an acknowledgment of receipt card so you can prove service.

If you are garnishing a bank account, you *must* serve the correct branch of the bank.

If you are garnishing wages, you have to serve the documents within seven days of pay day.

You must also serve a copy of the documents on the debtor, although you won't do that until after you've served the garnishee — to prevent the debtor from getting the money before you do. In practice, if your garnishment is unsuccessful because the garnishee doesn't have any money of the debtor's, you won't have to bother serving the debtor.

SAMPLE #20
GARNISHING ORDER AFTER JUDGMENT

GARNISHING ORDER (AFTER JUDGMENT)	IN THE PROVINCIAL COURT OF BRITISH COLUMBIA	Court File Number 9101112

PSC013
FORM 14
REV 07/85

_____ Richmond _____ Registry

BETWEEN: JORDAN HOMEOWNER   , JUDGMENT CREDITOR,

AND: ROBERTSON'S ROOFERS   , JUDGMENT DEBTOR,

AND: ROYAL BANK   , GARNISHEE

Before   Her Honour Judge Allan   : Judge/Registrar

On reading the affidavit of   Jordan Homeowner   , sworn the 15

day of   April   , 19 9–

I order that, except as otherwise ordered, all debts, obligations, and liabilities owing, payable, or accruing due from the garnishee (or garnishees or any of them) to the judgment debtor be attached up to the total amount set out below and paid into Court. Where any of the debts, obligations, and liabilities are owing, payable, or accruing due for wages or salary, then only so much of them as is permitted by Section 4 of the Court Order Enforcement Act are to be attached and paid into Court.
(See Reverse)

DATED the 2nd   day of   April   , 19 9–

TO THE JUDGMENT DEBTOR:
Name and address

Robertson's Roofers
2020 E. 7th Ave
Richmond, B.C.

By the Court (   )

TO THE GARNISHEE:
Name and address

Royal Bank
1032 Cambie Ave
Richmond, B.C.

TO THE JUDGMENT DEBTOR:
Name and address

	$	c
Amount due on Judgment or balance of it (as the case may be) _____	642	.20
Cost of attachment proceedings _____	25	.00
Total amount attached _____	667	.20

NOTICE TO GARNISHEE

If you do not pay into court at once the amount of your indebtedness to the defendant or judgment debtor, or the amount limited by the above attaching order, or if you do not dispute your liability, an order may be made against you for the payment of the full amount with costs.

If you dispute your liability you should at once file a dispute note, and the registrar will then send you notice of the day on which you are to appear in court.

"Owing, payable or accruing due" means owing, payable or accruing due at the time this order was served on you but, in the case of wages or salary, includes wages or salary that will, in the ordinary course of employment, become due and payable within 7 days after the day on which the affidavit first above mentioned was sworn.

NOTICE TO EMPLOYER

Section 29 of the Court Order Enforcement Act makes it an offence to dismiss or demote an employee or terminate a contract of employment of an employee solely by reason of the service of a garnishing order on the employer issued under this Act.

NOTICE TO DEFENDANT OR JUDGMENT DEBTOR

To prevent further garnishment proceedings you may apply to the registrar or the court and, if considered just in all the circumstances, an order may be made releasing all or part of this garnishment and providing for payment of the judgment against you by instalments. Court address is:

When making payment into Court, Court File No. must be quoted and made payable to Minister of Finance.
REGISTRY

(SEE REVERSE FOR ADDITIONAL INFORMATION)

SAMPLE #21
AFFIDAVIT IN SUPPORT
OF GARNISHING ORDER AFTER JUDGMENT

IN THE PROVINCIAL COURT OF BRITISH COLUMBIA

AFFIDAVIT IN SUPPORT
OF GARNISHING ORDER
AFTER JUDGMENT

COURT FILE NUMBER

9101112

PSC 014
FORM B
REV 01-85

_____ Richmond _____ Registry

BETWEEN   JORDAN HOMEOWNER   , JUDGMENT CREDITOR.

AND: ROBERTSON'S ROOFERS LTD.   , JUDGMENT DEBTOR.

I, __Jordan Homeowner, store clerk_____
(NAME, ADDRESS AND OCCUPATION)

make oath and say:

(1)   I am the person entitled to enforce the judgment or order referred to.
      Or
      (1)   I am the solicitor for the person entitled to enforce the judgment or order referred to.
      Or
      (1)   I am acting for the person entitled to enforce the judgment or order referred to, and I am aware of the facts referred to.
(2)   On a judgment entered (or order made, as the case may be) in this action, the Judgment Debtor was found
      to be indebted to the Judgment Creditor for $ _1042.20_____ and the
      whole of the sum still remains due (or and of which the sum of $ 642.20

      dollars still remains due, as the case may be), and the same is due and owing by the said   debtor
      to the said creditor   after making all just discounts.

(3)   That to the best of my information and belief

      __Royal Bank, 1032 Cambie Ave., Richmond, B.C._____, the garnishee,
      (NAME, ADDRESS, AND DESCRIPTION OF THE GARNISHEE)

      is indebted, under obligation, or liable to the Judgment Debtor, and that the said garnishee is in the jurisdiction
      of this Court.

SWORN before me at Richmond

Province of British Columbia, this 1st

        day of April   _Jordan Homeowner_
                                                      DEPONENT

   19 9–

J. M. Commissioner
A COMMISSIONER FOR TAKING AFFIDAVITS FOR BRITISH COLUMBIA

REGISTRY

3. If you are successful

As you will see from looking at the Garnishing Order (see Sample #20), the garnishee is required to pay the money not to you, but to the court. This is referred to as a "payment into court" or, sometimes just a "payment in."

This "payment in" is a protection for the debtor against having money wrongfully diverted. It gives the debtor a chance to either consent to the money being paid out to the creditor or to contest it.

There are three ways the creditor can get the money once it's been paid into court:

(a) If the original payment order was made in default (i.e., the defendant didn't file a Reply to the claim), the money will be paid to the creditor automatically three months after it was paid into court. The creditor simply has to file proof that the debtor was served with the garnishing order. It will probably also be necessary to call the registry and remind them when the three months is up.

(b) If the debtor signs a consent form, the money will be paid out immediately.

(c) The creditor serves a Notice of Payment Out on the debtor (see Sample #22). (This must be served in the same way as a summons, either personally or by registered mail.) This notice gives the debtor 10 days to file a Notice of Intention to Dispute the payment out (see Sample #23). (Note that the Notice of Intention to Dispute is not a special form; it is just a letter to the registrar explaining why the debtor objects to the payment of the money to the creditor.)

If the debtor does file this notice, both parties will be notified of a hearing date and a judge will decide what becomes of the money that was paid into court. If the debtor does not file a Notice of Intention to Dispute within ten days,

120

the creditor must file proof that the Notice of Payment Out and the Garnishing Order were properly served on the debtor. Then the money will be paid to the creditor.

The creditor's expenses for serving the forms will usually be added on to the money that the debtor owes. The registrar will estimate these at the time the Garnishing Order is filed, and add them to the total to be garnished. However, these will be recoverable only if the garnishment is at least partially successful; that is, if some amount of money is paid into court as a result.

4. If you are unsuccessful

There are three reasons why a garnishment might fail to produce any money at all:

(a) The documents may be faulty. For example, the name of the garnishee may be incorrect. In that case the garnishee is under no obligation to do anything.

(b) The documents may not be properly served. For example, they might go to the wrong branch of the debtor's bank, or they might be served on an employer two weeks before pay day.

(c) There may be no money available. The bank account may be closed or, for whatever reason, the garnishee may simply not have any money that is owing to the debtor.

If the garnishee takes the position that there is no money available, the creditor may have some reason to doubt this is true. If so, the creditor can apply to the court to have the garnishee examined before a judge. If you decide to take this step you should consider getting legal advice.

5. What can the debtor do?

A debtor who is subject to garnishment proceedings has three choices:

SAMPLE #22
NOTICE OF PAYMENT OUT

IN THE PROVINCIAL COURT OF BRITISH COLUMBIA

Court File Number

9101112

PSC 024
REV 8 83

_____ Richmond _____ REGISTRY

BETWEEN   JORDAN HOMEOWNER   JUDGEMENT CREDITOR

AND   ROBERTSON'S ROOFERS LTD.   JUDGEMENT DEBTOR

TAKE NOTICE that, under the Court Order Enforcement Act, the sum of

$ 600.00   paid into the Court by the Garnishee under the order

herein issued on the 1st   day of May   19 9~   . will
be paid out to the Judgement Creditor or his solicitor ten days after service of this notice, unless, on or before the
day on which the ten days expires, you file with the undersigned notice of your intention to dispute the payment out.

DATED the   2nd   day of   May   .199~

I. M. Registrar
By the Court (_____)

ADDRESS OF COURT
6931 Granville Ave
Richmond, B.C.

(Name, address & telephone no. of Judgement Creditor)

Jordan Homeowner
123 W. 4th Ave
Surrey, B.C.
V2E 3B2
696-2166

To the above-named Judgement Debtor:
(name, address & telephone no.)

Roberson's Roofers Ltd.
2020 E. 7th Ave
Richmond, B.C.
V3I 3B2

REGISTRY

122

NOTICE OF INTENTION TO DISPUTE

TO: The Registrar, Small Claims Court
FROM: Robertson's Roofers Ltd.

RE: Action #9101112

NOTICE OF INTENTION TO DISPUTE

*Money was paid into court on April 3, 199- by Robertson's Roofers
pursuant to a Garnishing Order obtained by John Homeowner on April 2,
199-. I dispute the payment of any of this money to John Homeowner on
the grounds that (enter reasons).*

(a) Ignore the whole thing. In three months the money
will be paid to the creditor. If it is enough to cover the
whole amount that is owing, that will be the end of it.
Otherwise, there are likely to be other enforcement
proceedings.

(b) Contact the creditor and work out an arrangement for
payment of the debt. This might involve signing a
consent form that lets the creditor have the money
immediately and then agreeing to instalments to pay
the balance, if any.

(c) Ask the registrar to schedule a payment hearing so
that the judge can order a payment schedule. If that
happens, then as long as the debtor makes the payments as ordered, the creditor cannot garnish again
or take any other enforcement action.

b. SEIZURE OF GOODS

Another course of action is to have a bailiff take possession of goods belonging to the debtor, and sell them at public auction. Any proceeds, after payment of the bailiff's costs, will go to you.

The rules about seizure of goods are contained in the Court Order Enforcement Act.

1. What can be seized?

Here again, it will pay to do some research and find out something about the debtor's situation. Does he or she have goods that would be worth seizing? If the debtor isn't someone you have regular dealings with, or know well, a payment hearing is your best opportunity to find out what might be available for seizure.

The debtor is allowed to choose $2 000 worth of items to be exempt from seizure. He or she can do this at the time of the seizure, or within 48 hours after. However, a "trader" may not claim as an exemption any of the goods and merchandise that form part of the stock-in-trade of his or her business. In other words, a store owner cannot claim an exemption for part of the store's inventory.

If you plan to seize a car, you will need to know the legal owner. You can find out by writing to:

Motor Vehicle Branch
Attn: Vehicle Records
2631 Douglas Street
Victoria, B.C.
V8T 5A3

Alternatively, you can leave it to the bailiff to get the information, but you will have to pay for this.

Banks and finance companies often have chattel mortgages against vehicles and other major items. (This means that the lender has a legal interest in the item until the "owner" has paid off the balance.) Anything that has a chattel mort-

124

gage or other encumbrance against it may only be seized if the debtor's equity is greater than the amount owed under the court order.

You can find out about encumbrances against items other than motor vehicles by writing to:

Corporate, Central & Mobile Home Registry
2nd floor, 940 Blanshard Street
Victoria, B.C.
V8W 3E6

Anything that the debtor owns *jointly* with someone else, may not be seized.

Cash may be seized and will be handed over to the creditor. Promissory notes, bonds, and other securities may also be seized, as can shares in a public company (a company trading on a stock exchange). Shares in a private company generally may not be seized.

If the debtor owns a mortgage, that is, if someone is paying money on a mortgage to the debtor, that mortgage can be seized. The mortgagor will then be notified to make all payments to the sheriff until the judgment is satisfied. The sheriff, of course, pays the money to the creditor, after deducting the sheriff's expenses.

2. How to do it

Ask at the Small Claims registry for a Order for Seizure and Sale (see Sample #24). When you return the completed form, be prepared to provide any information you have about the debtor's goods and where they are located. If you have written to the motor vehicle branch, for example, provide a copy of the reply. The more information you can provide, the better.

You will have to pay a deposit to cover the estimated cost of seizing the goods and selling them. If the proceeds of sale are sufficient, you will be able to add this cost to the amount you recover from the debtor. But be aware that if the attempt

ORDER FOR SEIZURE AND SALE
IN THE PROVINCIAL COURT OF BRITISH COLUMBIA (SMALL CLAIMS COURT)

REGISTRY FILE NUMBER
9101112
REGISTRY LOCATION
Richmond

FORM 11 (RULE 11)
SCL 011 (11 90)

Fill in the name, address and telephone number of the person who is named as the creditor in the Payment or Default Order.

NAME Jordan Homeowner
ADDRESS 123 W. 4th Ave

CREDITOR

CITY, TOWN, MUNICIPALITY Surrey   B.C. PROV   V2E 3B2 POSTAL CODE   TEL 686-2166

Fill in the name, address and telephone number of the person who is named as the debtor in the Payment or Default Order.

NAME Robertson's Roofers Ltd.
ADDRESS 2020 E. 7th Ave

DEBTOR

CITY, TOWN, MUNICIPALITY Richmond   B.C. PROV   V3I 2C4 POSTAL CODE   TEL 378-1230

To the sheriff or court bailiff:

You are ordered to seize any goods of the debtor named in attached order that are not exempted from seizure under the *Court Order Enforcement Act*, and to sell them by public auction, sealed bid or any other similar method in order to realize your fees and disbursements for enforcing this order and the **TOTAL AMOUNT DUE TO THE CREDITOR** calculated as follows:

(a) Total Amount of Payment or Default Order	$	1042.20
(b) Less any payments to the creditor	− $	500.00
	= $	542.20

If claiming interest, attach a sheet showing your calculations

(c) plus interest calculated to the date this order is issued	+ $	6.00
(d) plus enforcement expenses allowed by the Court to the date this order is issued	+ $	75.00
TOTAL	= $	623.20

If you want to be allowed expenses under line (e), submit them to the registrar. They might include search fees at the motor vehicle or personal property registry.

(e) plus any expenses allowed by the Court in relation to this order	+ $	10.00
DEPOSIT PAID for Sheriff or Court bailiff's fees and disbursements	+ $	100.00
TOTAL AMOUNT DUE TO THE CREDITOR at the date this order is issued	= $	733.20

Then deduct from the proceeds of sale your **ACTUAL FEES AND DISBURSEMENTS** for enforcing this order. From the balance, pay to the creditor the **TOTAL AMOUNT DUE TO THE CREDITOR**. Then pay any balance remaining after that to the debtor.

Attach a copy of the payment or default order you are enforcing.

A copy of the payment or default order is attached.

Issued on:

month   day   year   by the court

This order remains in force for one year after the date it was issued by the Court.

What is exempt from seizure?
You may not seize anything that the debtor owns jointly with someone else.
Also, the debtor can choose $2,000 worth of goods to be exempt from seizure. This can be done at the time of the seizure or within 48 hours.

sheriff / court bailiff copy

ORDER FOR SEIZURE AND SALE

sheriff / court bailiff copy

at seizure is unsuccessful, or the proceeds are insufficient, you will be stuck with the costs.

The bailiff eventually will return the Order for Seizure and Sale to the registry with a notation explaining the outcome.

3. What can the debtor do?

The debtor will be given the opportunity, at the time of the seizure, to pay the amount owing on the judgment. If the judgment is not paid, the debtor may select the $2 000 worth of goods to be exempt from seizure. If this isn't done at the time of seizure, the debtor can contact the sheriff within 48 hours to retrieve the exempt goods.

The debtor also always has the option of asking for a payment hearing. At that time a payment schedule could be ordered, which would protect the debtor from further collection proceedings.

c. REGISTRATION AGAINST LAND

Land, or real estate, cannot be seized in the way that personal property can, but it can be used in the collection process if the debtor owns any.

A creditor who holds a judgment against any land owner can register that judgment in the Land Title Office. This will prevent the owner from mortgaging, selling, or dealing in any way with the land without first paying the judgment.

A judgment *can* be registered against property that is owned jointly by the debtor and another person. (A family home is often owned jointly by husband and wife, for example.) However, if the debtor dies, the property goes to the surviving joint owner and the registration will be cancelled.

1. How to do it

Get a Certificate of Judgment from the Small Claims registry (see Sample #25). There is a nominal fee for this. Take the certificate to the Land Title Office for the area where the land is. Ask the staff there for the necessary forms and fill them out. You can register the judgment against more than one property if you wish. There will be a small fee for each registration.

Then, you may simply wait. If someone knows that there is a judgment registered against his or her land, they will probably try to get rid of it, by paying the judgment. However, you don't have to wait forever. You may at any time go to court to force a sale of the property. If the property were sold, your judgment would be paid from the proceeds. But this application is to the Supreme Court and will likely require a lawyer. Be sure the stakes are high enough to make it worth the effort and expense of taking this route.

If you do decide to wait, remember that the registration will only last for two years. At that time you will have to ask for a new certificate and file it again.

d. SENDING THE DEBTOR TO JAIL

If you have a payment schedule already and the debtor has not lived up to it, you can have a default hearing. As a last resort, if the debtor simply refuses to pay, the judge at a default hearing can send the debtor to jail.

1. The default hearing

A creditor can ask the registrar to schedule a default hearing if the payment schedule that is in default was ordered either:

- (a) at a settlement conference,
- (b) with the creditor's agreement at the end of a trial,
- (c) after a payment hearing, or
- (d) after an application to change the terms of a payment schedule.

Obviously, this covers most situations. It means that the default hearing is available as long as the payment schedule was set after some consideration by a judge.

128

SAMPLE #25
CERTIFICATE OF JUDGMENT

Court File Number
45678

In the Provincial Court of British Columbia

Held at Prince George ; Small Claims Act

BETWEEN: ROBIN GARDINER

, JUDGMENT CREDITOR

AND: LESLIE HOUSEHOLDER

, JUDGMENT DEBTOR

Certificate of Judgment

I, the undersigned Registrar of the said Court, do hereby certify that on the 15th

day of January , A.D. 19 9¬

the above-mentioned Creditor obtained a Judgment against Leslie Householder

, the Debtor in the above-mentioned

Court, for the sum of $ 246.30 , and $ 35.00 costs, making together the

sum of $ 281.30

As witness my hand, this 16 day of January , A.D. 19 9–.

J.B. Registrar

Registrar

2. How to ask for a default hearing

A creditor simply has to ask the registry for a Summons to a Default Hearing, fill it out and file it (see Sample #26). The sheriff will serve it at least seven days before the hearing. There is no charge to the creditor.

If the debtor has records or other documents that may be relevant, the summons can include a requirement that those be brought to the hearing.

If the debtor is a company, any officer, director, or employee may be named in the summons. If the debtor is a partnership, one of the partners will be summoned.

3. What happens at the hearing?

The judge will ask the debtor questions to try to determine whether there is any legitimate reason for the failure to pay the judgment. The creditor will be allowed to respond to what the debtor says and to describe the efforts that have been made to enforce the judgment.

After listening to both sides, the judge may confirm the terms of the payment schedule already in effect, or change its terms in whatever way the judge thinks is fair.

If the judge decides that the debtor's explanation for not paying amounts to contempt of court — in other words, if he or she simply refuses to obey the court order — the judge can send the person to jail for up to 20 days.

If that happens, you will have to supply details of the amount that was originally ordered, the amount that has been paid, and the amount still owing, including interest. These figures go on a Warrant of Imprisonment (see Sample #27), and you will sign it, certifying that the amounts are true, so you should be prepared to supply them.

The sheriff who goes to arrest the debtor will give him or her a chance to pay the full amount to avoid going to jail. Once

SAMPLE #26
SUMMONS TO A DEFAULT HEARING

SUMMONS TO A DEFAULT HEARING
IN THE PROVINCIAL COURT OF BRITISH COLUMBIA (SMALL CLAIMS COURT)

REGISTRY FILE NUMBER
45678

REGISTRY LOCATION
Prince George

FORM 14 (RULE 13)
SCL 014 (11 90)

TO:
What is the name and address of the person you are requiring to come to court?

NAME Leslie Householder
ADDRESS 789 Main Street

CITY TOWN MUNICIPALITY Prince George   B.C. PROV   V6K 2M3 POSTAL CODE   TEL # 378-5678

Because the debtor has not obeyed the payment schedule in the attached order, you are summoned to a default hearing in the case between:

Copy the names of all parties in the case as shown on the Payment Order.

ROBIN GARDINER   CREDITOR

and

LESLIE HOUSEHOLDER   DEBTOR

Fill in the date, time and place of the hearing.

You are required to attend the Provincial Court of British Columbia

on   April _month_   23 _day_   199– _year_   at   10 _time_   A M   or as soon after this time as the court schedule allows.

at   1600 3rd Ave, Prince George _court location_

List what you want the person to bring.

You are required to bring the following records and other things:

All books and records relating to your financial situation, including bank statements for 1991 and 1992 and income tax returns for 1990 and 1991.

Attach a copy of the Payment Order.

I certify that the debtor named in the attached order has not obeyed the payment schedule in the order.

Fill in the date and sign here.

April _month_   6 _day_   199– _year_   _Robin Gardiner_ signature of creditor

What happens at a default hearing?
At a default hearing, the judge may
   a) confirm the terms of a payment schedule or other order, or
   b) change the terms of a payment schedule or other order in any manner that the judge thinks is fair to the debtor and the creditor.
The judge may also issue a warrant for the imprisonment of the debtor, if
   a) the debtor has not obeyed a payment schedule, and
   b) the debtor's explanation, or failure to give an explanation, of why the payment schedule has not been obeyed is considered by the judge to amount to contempt of court.

What happens if you do not attend?
The judge may issue a warrant for your arrest.

month   _day_   _year_   _by the court_

court copy

the debtor is arrested, the warrant can still be cancelled at any time by payment of the full amount.

A person can be arrested under a Warrant of Imprisonment for up to one year after it is issued. If more than one year goes by, a new warrant will have to be issued before the debtor can be arrested.

This is not a case of debtor's prison. The person is not being jailed for owing money. The penalty is for contempt of court. Whether it is applied or not will be very much a question of the judge's assessment of the debtor's attitude.

If the debtor is sent to jail, there is no charge to the creditor. It also does not excuse the debt. The amount is still owing to the creditor after the debtor has served the jail term. The debtor, however, always has the option of paying the money and if he or she does so, will be released from jail.

e. SUMMARY

There are a number of options available to a creditor who has a Small Claims Court judgment against someone who hasn't paid. You should consider —

(a) garnishment of the debtor's wages or bank account or any other money that may be owing to him or her;

(b) seizure of goods belonging to the debtor, such as an automobile or household goods;

(c) registration of the judgment against any real estate the debtor may own; or

(d) ask for a default hearing where the issue of payment will be examined by a judge.

To decide which option presents the best chance of getting your money for you, you need information about the debtor's financial situation. A payment hearing is a good place to get that information.

The debtor who is faced with any of these collection proceedings has options as well. Usually the best approach is to contact the creditor, or ask the court for a payment hearing, and try to work out a payment schedule that you can manage.

SAMPLE #27
WARRANT OF IMPRISONMENT

WARRANT OF IMPRISONMENT
IN THE PROVINCIAL COURT OF BRITISH COLUMBIA (SMALL CLAIMS COURT)

FORM 15 (RULE 13)
SCL 015 (11/90)

REGISTRY FILE NUMBER
45678
REGISTRY LOCATION
Prince George

In the case between:
ROBIN GARDINER

and

LESLIE HOUSEHOLDER

To all sheriffs and peace officers in British Columbia and to the director of the correctional centre referred to below:

This Court orders that | Leslie Householder | be arrested and
name of person to be imprisoned

taken to | Lower Mainland Regional | and imprisoned for | 3 | days
correctional centre

for contempt of Court [X] under Rule 13(8) of the Small Claims Rules.
 [ ] under Rule 19(1) of the Small Claims Rules.

Issued on:

May _month_ | 30 _day_ | 199- _year_ | *I. M. Registrar* _the court_

This part must be completed if the warrant is for the imprisonment of a debtor under Rule 13(8).

Where the warrant is issued under section 13(8) of the Small Claims Rules:

(a) Total Amount of Payment Order ... $ 281.30

(b) Less any payments to the creditor ... − $ 0

(c) Amount remaining due ... = $ 281.30

If claiming interest, show your calculations. Attach an extra sheet if necessary.

(d) Interest (calculated to the date below) ... + $ 4.80

(e) Creditor's expenses allowed by the Court ... + $ 25.00

Amount due to creditor **TOTAL** = $ 311.10

If the TOTAL is paid to the Registrar before the debtor is arrested, the warrant will be cancelled. If the TOTAL is paid after the arrest of the debtor, to the Registrar or the person who has custody of the debtor, the warrant will be cancelled.

I certify these figures to be true.

May _month_ | 30 _day_ | 199- _year_ | *Robin Gardiner* _signature of creditor_

This warrant remains in force for 1 year after the date it was issued by the Court.

court copy

court copy

134

GLOSSARY

ADJOURN

To put off, defer, postpone; to postpone a settlement conference, trial, or application until another specified time, or indefinitely.

ADMISSION

A voluntary agreement by a party that certain facts are true.

AFFIDAVIT

Written or printed statement of facts, confirmed by the oath or affirmation of the party making it, taken before someone with authority to administer an oath, such as a notary public or a lawyer.

CLAIMANT

A person who brings an action (files a Notice of Claim).

CONTRIBUTORY NEGLIGENCE

A claimant's failure to meet the standard of conduct necessary for his or her own protection, which, together with the defendant's actions, contributes to the particular harm complained of.

COUNTERCLAIM

A claim presented by a defendant in opposition to a Notice of Claim. A claim by a defendant against a claimant.

DAMAGES

Compensation for loss, injury, or deterioration to someone's person or property caused by the negligence, design, or accident of someone else.

DEBT

A sum of money due as a consequence of some contract or agreement where the amount is fixed and specific and does not depend on any valuation by the court to settle it.

DEFAULT ORDER

May be obtained by the claimant if the defendant fails to file a Reply or to appear at trial; may be obtained by a defendant who has filed a counterclaim if the plaintiff fails to appear at the trial.

DEFENDANT

The person defending or denying; the party against whom relief or recovery is sought in an action.

GARNISHEE

Someone, such as an employer or a bank, who has money or property belonging to a defendant, or who owes money to the defendant, and who is served with a notice to pay it to the court until the result of a lawsuit is determined.

GARNISHMENT

A legal notice to a garnishee ordering him or her not to pay the money or deliver the property of the defendant to the defendant but to deliver it to the court until the result of a lawsuit is determined.

GARNISHOR

The person who issues a garnishing order.

HEARSAY

Evidence that is merely the repetition of statements made by others. Because of the weaknesses of this kind of evidence, it is admitted only in specified cases.

JUDGMENT CREDITOR

One who has obtained a Payment Order against a debtor.

JUDGMENT DEBTOR

A person against whom a Payment Order has been made.

LEADING QUESTIONS

Questions that suggest the "right" answer to a witness.

LIBEL

Written words that are untrue and tend to lower a person's reputation in the minds of others.

LIMITATION PERIOD

The time limit for starting a lawsuit.

MALICIOUS PROSECUTION

Prosecution or a lawsuit brought in bad faith with no reasonable expectation that it could succeed.

ORDER FOR SEIZURE AND SALE

Court order used by a judgment creditor to send the sheriff to seize the property of the judgment debtor.

SLANDER

Spoken words that are untrue and tend to lower a person's reputation in the minds of others.

SUBSTITUTED SERVICE

Service of a document by some means other than the normal procedures and authorized by an order of the court.

THIRD PARTY NOTICE

A notice by a defendant to join another party in the lawsuit. The third party is then in the position similar to that of a defendant. The notice must be served as if it were a Notice of Claim.

APPENDIX
SMALL CLAIMS REGISTRIES

Abbotsford
33203 South Fraser Way
Clearbrook, B.C.
V2T 1W6
853-5911

Aldergrove (see Surrey)

Ashcroft
P.O. Box 639
Ashcroft, B.C.
V0K 1A0
453-9174

Bella Bella
RCMP
757-2388
(Radio Operator)

Bella Coola
RCMP
P.O. Box 125
Bella Coola, B.C.
V0T 1C0
799-5533

Burnaby
6263 Deer Lake Avenue
Burnaby, B.C.
V5G 1J0
660-7135

Blue River
P.O. Box 81
Blue River, B.C.
V0E 1J0
673-8334

Burns Lake
508 Yellowhead Highway
Burns Lake, B.C.
V0J 1E0
692-3228

Campbell River
Courthouse
500 - 13th Avenue
Campbell River, B.C.
V9W 6P1
286-7510

Chase
P.O. Box 581
2186 Shuswap Avenue
Chase, B.C.
V0E 1MO
679-3024

Chilliwack
9391 College Street
Chilliwack, B.C.
V2P 4L7
795-8347

Clearwater
P.O. Box 1981
RR #1
363 Mirtle Crescent
Clearwater, B.C.
V0E 1N0
674-2113

Courtney
Provincial Court
420 Cumberland
Courtney, B.C.
V9N 8H5
334-1120

Coquitlam
2165 Kelly Avenue
Coquitlam, B.C.
V3C 4W6
941-0604

Cranbrook
102 - 11th Avenue S.
Cranbrook, B.C.
V1C 2P3
426-1234

Creston
238 - 1017 Vancouver Street
Creston, B.C.
V0B 1G0
428-3200

Dawson Creek
V1G 4J2
784-2278

Delta
4465 Clarence Taylor Crescent
Delta, B.C.
V4K 3W4
660-3121

Duncan
Registry Law Courts
238 Government Street
Duncan, B.C.
V9L 1A5
746-1242

Fernie
P.O. Box 1800
401 Fourth Avenue
Fernie, B.C.
V0B 1M0
423-4601

Fort Nelson
Bag 1000
Fort Nelson, B.C.
V0C 1R0

Fort St.John
Courthouse
10600 - 100th Street
Fort St. John, B.C.
V1J 4L6
787-3231

Golden
Courthouse
606 - 6th Street N.
Box 1500
Golden, B.C.
V0A 1H0
344-7581

Grand Forks
524 Central Avenue
Box 1059
Grand Forks, B.C.
V0H 1H0
442-5464

Haney (see Maple Ridge)

Hope
999 Water Street
Box 610
Hope, B.C.
V0X 1L0
869-9958

100 Mile House
V0K 2E0
395-5562

Pemberton
V0N 2L0
894-6663

Invermere
P.O. Box 725
645 - 7th Avenue
Invermere, B.C.
861-7260

Kamloops
223 - 455 Columbia Street
Kamloops, B.C.
V2C 6K4
828-4344

Kelowna
1420 Water Street
Kelowna, B.C.
V1A 3A2
861-7260

Kimberley
1565 Victoria Avenue
Kimberley, B.C.
V1A 3A2
427-4836

Kitimat
603 City Centre
Kitimat, B.C.
V8C 2N1
632-4781

Langley
20389 Fraser Highway
Langley, B.C.
V3A 4E9
530-1164

Lillooet
615 Main Street
Lillooet, B.C.
V0K 1V0
256-7445

Lytton
P.O. Box 310
256 - 6th Avenue
Lytton, B.C.
V0K 1Z0
455-2255

MacKenzie
Box 2050
64 Centennial Drive
MacKenzie, B.C.
V0J 2C0
997-3377

Maple Ridge
11960 Haney Road
Maple Ridge, B.C.
V2X 6G1
467-1515

Masset
(Queen Charlotte Islands)
P.O. Box 230
1644 Main Street
Masset, B.C.
V0T 1M0
626-5512

Matsqui
33203 South Fraser Way
Clearbrook, B.C.
V2T 1X1
852-5330

Merritt
1840 Nicola Avenue
Merritt, B.C.
V0K 1R0
378-9350

Nakusp
Box 328
415 Broadway
Nakusp, B.C.
V0G 1R0
265-4253

Nanaimo
Courthouse
35 Front Street
Nanaimo, B.C.
V9R 5J1
755-2448

Nelson
Courthouse
320 Ward Street
Nelson, B.C.
V1L 1S6
354-6165

New Westminster
Law Courts
Begbie Square
New Westminster, B.C.
V3M 1C9
660-8501

North Vancouver
200 East 23rd Avenue
North Vancouver, B.C.
V7L 4R4
980-0591

Ocean Falls
RCMP
P.O. Box 590
Ocean Falls, B.C.
V0T 1P0
289-3311

Oliver
Courthouse
P.O. Box 1350
Oliver, B.C.
V0H 1T0
498-4345

100 Mile House
P.O. Box 1060
272 5th Avenue
100 Mile House, B.C.
V0K 2E0
295-5562

Penticton
Courthouse
100 Main Street
Penticton, B.C.
V2A 5A5
492-1231

Port Alberni
Courthouse
2999 - 4th Avenue
Port Alberni, B.C.
V9Y 4M9
724-5741

Port Hardy
Courthouse
8755 Granville Street
Port Hardy, B.C.
V0N 2P0
949-6122

Powell River
Courthouse
6953 Alberni Street
Powell River, B.C.
V8A 2B8
485-2861

Prince George
1600 Third Avenue
Prince George, B.C.
V2L 3G6
565-6070

Prince Rupert
100 Market Place
Prince Rupert, B.C.
V8J 1B7
627-0525

Princeton
Courthouse
151 Vermillion
P.O. Box 1210
Princeton, B.C.
V0X 1W0
295-3113

Quesnel
Courthouse
1123 2nd Street W.
Box 2130
Revelstoke, B.C.
V0E 2S0
837-7654

Richmond
6931 Granville Avenue
Richmond, B.C.
V7C 4M9
660-4693

Rossland
Courthouse
2288 Columbia Avenue
Box 639
Rossland, B.C.
V0G 1Y0
362-7368

Salmon Arm
Courthouse
20 W Hudson Street
Box 1990
Salmon Arm, B.C.
V0E 2T0
832-1610

Sechelt
5589 Wharf Avenue
P.O. Box 160
Sechelt, B.C.
V0N 3A0
885-5804

Smithers
3793 Alfred Street
Box 2239
Smithers, B.C.
V0J 2N0
847-7376

Squamish
38073 2nd Avenue
Box 37
Squamish, B.C.
V0N 3G0
892-5911

Stewart
Court House
Box 127
Stewart, B.C.
V0T 1W0
636-2294

Surrey
144340 - 57th Avenue
Surrey, B.C.
V3T 4K4
572-2210

Terrace
3408 Kalum Street
Terrace, B.C.
V8G 2N6
638-3242

Valemount
P.O. Box 125
28 Dogwood
Valemount, B.C.
V0E 2Z0
566-4652

Vancouver
814 Richards Street
Vancouver, B.C.
V6B 3A7
660-2466

Vanderhoof
P.O. Box 1220
Vanderhoof, B.C.
V0J 3A0
567-6330

Vernon
Courthouse
3001 - 27th Street
Vernon, B.C.
V1T 4W5
549-5422

Victoria
Law Courts Building
850 Burdett Avenue
Victoria, B.C.
V8W 1B4
387-1478

Williams Lake
540 Borland Street
Williams Lake, B.C.
V2G 1R8
398-4307